NEW IDENTITY

30 Days of Prayer for Spiritual Transformation

For more from Adam Narciso, visit www.adamnarciso.com

ISBN-13: 978-1-7327978-0-2

WHAT IS *NEW IDENTITY*?

New Identity is a 30-day prayer journey designed to establish you in your identity in Christ. Each day consists of the following parts:

INTRODUCTION
A personal presentation of a transformative truth about you.

SCRIPTURES FOR MEDITATION
3-5 scriptures affirming who God says you are.

REFLECTION & RESPONSE
Questions, prayer steps and practical action to engage your new identity.

DECLARATION
A declarative prayer to recite out loud.

The *New Identity* prayer journey culminates on Day 30, when you follow a template to write your own Personal Identity Declaration. *New Identity* engages you in the core discipleship themes of Catalyst Ministries:

The Great Commandment
Love God with everything.

The Great Conformity
Become like Jesus in every way.

The Great Commission
Make disciples everywhere.

To the great multitude who have yet to be swept into the Father's arms. May you discover who you are in Christ and live from those truths far sooner than the generation before you.

ENDORSEMENTS

I really loved Adam Narciso's book, New Identity! It's simple but profound and timeless in content. As a missionary and church planter this is the type of book that I want to be taking my church through to make sure that the foundation for their spiritual life is solid. The truths in this book in terms of understanding our identity in God will bring life-changing transformation to the reader. I highly recommend *New Identity* to leaders, new believers, or those wanting to strengthen foundational truths in their lives. Excellent job Adam!

Jennifer Roberts
Co-Founder, Florianopolis House of Prayer
Florianopolis, Brasil

This is a powerful tool in the hands of believers in all stages of sanctification. Adam does an excellent job helping Scripture come alive in simple and effective ways. This devotional will change your life if you allow the Holy Spirit to work in your heart and mind. I especially appreciate the practical application that Adam provides with each lesson. This resource is thorough and useful in growing and breaking through strongholds and lies of the enemy in numerous facets of the believer's life. I wholeheartedly encourage everyone to take a deep dive into this life-changing tool.

Darrin Miller
National Director, City Life
Youth for Christ, USA

Adam truly is a man who carries authority and history with God. His heart for people knowing God and finding his truth real in their lives is so the heart of Jesus!

Brian Barcelona
Founder & CEO, One Voice Student Missions
Pasadena, CA USA

The danger today in our walk with Christ is attempting to skip the journey and settle for the quick zap of microwave spirituality. New Identity is a sure guide by a tried, tested, and proven traveler. Through brief personal illustrations, penetrating questions, pertinent Scripture, and spot-on reflection questions for practical application, Narciso enables the reader to establish his and her God-given identity in Christ. The daily declarations embolden the heart. As Narciso says, "From our identity flows our behavior, our lifestyle and ultimately, our calling."

Dr. Bill Heth
Professor of Greek & Biblical Studies, Taylor University
Upland, IN USA

Adam Narciso brilliantly and effectively takes the reader on a 30-day journey into the truth, destiny, and assurance of who we, as children of God and the Bride of Christ, were created to be. Adam writes with intense vulnerability from his own journey. He also gives a treasury of practical application from Scripture as to how we can operate in our divine identities and invite others to that same high call. As his friend, and as one who has sat under his teaching, I could not more highly recommend Adam's book *New Identity*. Say yes to this journey and discover who you really are in Christ.

Matt Gilman
Worship Leader, Singer & Songwriter
Influence Music

I was very pleased to see the spectrum Adam covers in *New Identity*, from the very beginning of the discipleship journey, to the local church and beyond. I believe this book will be extremely useful to so many, especially those starting out in the Christian walk. All I could think about in my reading is using it here in Columbia, especially with a man I am discipling who I know would benefit from this material.

Ruth J. Ruibal, M.P. H., D. Hum., D. Min.
President, Julio C. Ruibal Ministries
Cali, Columbia

What a timely resource on who we are in Christ. Understanding and walking in the whole issue of identity (who Jesus is, who we are & whose we are) is so central if God's church is to be filled to the measure of all the fullness of God. As I read Adam's devotional, many times I had to stop as the Spirit was at work in my reading – encouraging, convicting, renewing. The Personal Identity Declaration Template is something I will return to again and again. Actually, I will go back to the whole devotional again and again. I'd recommend it for personal devotion and an exercise whole groups could do.

Seán Byrne
Co-Senior Pastor, Dublin Vineyard Church
Dublin, Ireland

Adam has written a timely workbook with a wonderful compilation of biblical revelations and insights on the theme of one's identity which will, without a doubt, transform people's lives. This manual is not a product of academic exercise, but from the experiences of a seasoned shepherd who has been involved in the spiritual contest to set the captives free by the power of the gospel.

Rev. Samuel Lee
Pastor, Tacoma Central Presbyterian Church
Lakewood, WA USA

Jesus told us that *out of the overflow of the heart the mouth speaks.* That's what I think of when I read Adam Narciso's *New Identity.* As a friend of 22 years, I have had the honor of seeing up close and personal the anointing, passion and desire of Adam's life and ministry to equip and empower people towards their God-given identity and purpose. This book is an overflow of insight, revelation and power because it's not just words on a page but the work of Christ lived out in humble and faithful man. *New Identity* isn't for those who want to gain more information (just hop on google for that); it is for those who want to take intentional steps toward understanding who they are in Christ. It's for those who don't want to trade the treasure of their significance in Christ for the trinkets of success, a ministry platform or social media likeability. If you want to be crystal clear about who you are so that you never doubt *why* you are, then read this book. Like, now!

Pat McFall
Campus Pastor
New Hope Hawaii Kai

In this hour, I believe that God is restoring His children's inheritance and understanding of the power of the gospel of Jesus Christ. That's what Adam has developed in *New Identity*, to bring change to the core beliefs that everyone has about themselves. This book does not just come from an intellectual knowledge of the Bible but from a man who has lived these truths out and been in the trenches for many years of ministry to see life after life find liberty in Christ. *New Identity* is an equipping manual with great stories, Bible studies, foundational gospel doctrine and tools for freedom from destructive cycles and spiritual bondages. I am happy to recommend this book and even more to recommend the ministry of my friend, Adam Narciso. I have seen the great fruit of Adam's preaching, training and prophetic ministry in various capacities. He is down to earth, an anointed communicator and carries a heart for the church to be grounded in the gospel.

John Hammer
Pastor, Sunrise Christian Center
Co-Founder of Represent Movement
Everett, WA USA

Adam Narciso speaks with authority on the topics of freedom, identity and the heart of the Father. His willingness to share his personal story and insight, alongside Scripture, will help each of us journey through our own stories into deeper intimacy with God. *New Identity* takes readers on a 30-day journey of discovering who they are in Christ. Adam is a trusted guide on this journey.

Scott Hayes
Lead Pastor, Element Church
East Lansing, MI USA

With quiet grace and powerful anointing Adam distills years of solid Gospel ministry to remind us *who we are* and *whose we are* as followers of Jesus. This Devotional echoes the invitation of our Lord to *know* Him, *be* like Him, and *do* what He says. Life cannot be more exciting than that: journeying with Jesus. I cannot more heartily endorse a guide for your 30 Day Journey as my friend and ministry partner, Adam Narciso.

Matthew Philip
Director of Global Outreach, Trinity Church
Former Associate Director of Urbana,
InterVarsity's Missions Conference

TABLE OF CONTENTS

FOREWORD

Identity is the very core of what it means to be human. Everything in life flows from our sense of identity. In contemporary culture, the identity question is front and center, and the assumption is that each of us is free to *choose* our identity.

But the unforeseen consequence of assuming that we *can* choose our identity has put a great deal of pressure on many people. For it's not simply trying out various identities that might please us, but figuring out which identities please others. So, we end up putting on all kinds of masks and personas, trying this identity or that, hoping to find the one which most fulfills us *and* gains the approval from others. And all this can leave us confused and disillusioned.

One of the great truths of the gospel is that you don't have to go looking for who you are; you can receive the everlasting love of God and *in that love,* discover who you are by what God says about you. And this leads to a life of peace, security, and freedom.

In *New Identity: 30 Days of Prayer for Spiritual Transformation,* Adam Narciso has written one of the best treatments of our God-given identity that I have ever seen. It is part devotional, part Bible study, part prayer guide, and *all* transformational. The daily readings are laced with richly textured stories that magnify each truth of who we are in Christ.

The uniqueness of this prayer guide lies not only in its comprehensive overview of our God-given identity, but in the way it's laid out; leading us as readers on a spiritual journey – through spiritual exercises and reflections – designed to change our thinking at its core. If you are familiar with *The Spiritual Exercises of Saint Ignatius*, then you know how powerful a guided prayer journey can be.

And what Narciso does so well in directing us on this journey, is give us mental hooks on which we can hang these identity statements, so that *remembering* how God sees us becomes second nature.

This 30-day spiritual journey will transform you. It will enable you to systematically disable the structure of lies that controls the human mind – and free you to discover who you really are, and who God has made you to be.

So, *take the journey!* And your life will flower into the most amazing destiny you could possibly imagine.

Steven Fry
President, Messenger Fellowship

INTRODUCTION

God has always been in the business of identity change. In fact, He has a track record of interrupting people's brokenness with the announcement of their new identity. He came to Abram, a childless senior citizen, and called him the father of a mighty nation (Gen. 12:1–3). He stood in Gideon's fear-filled hideout and called him a *mighty warrior* (Judg. 6:12). He called Peter *the rock* (Matt. 16:18) and Nathanael *a true Israelite without deceit* (John 1:47). Saul, the ruthless persecutor, became known as *Paul, the bondservant of Christ* (Rom. 1:1). Jesus chose fishermen, religious zealots and tax collectors—all sinners and redefined them, calling them *His disciples.*

The Christian life begins with an identity change. Sinners are declared saints, slaves are declared free, the fatherless are declared adopted and even those with the darkest resumes of sin are declared the very righteousness of Christ. God starts with changing our identity because from our identity flows our behavior, our lifestyle and ultimately, our calling.

"For our sake He made him to be sin who knew no sin, so that in Him we might become the righteousness of God." (2 Cor. 5:20).

Spiritual identity change is immediate and decisive; grace is radical. However, the transformation it produces in us is a journey— one marked by continually turning from our own way and looking straight at Jesus.

"But when one turns to the Lord, the veil is removed. Now the Lord is the Spirit, and where the Spirit of the Lord is, there is freedom. And we all, with unveiled face, beholding the glory of the Lord, are being transformed into the same image from one degree of glory to another. For this comes from the Lord who is the Spirit." (2 Cor. 3:16–18).

To turn from ourselves and behold Him is to become like Him. When we behold Him, He tells us who we really are.

MY TRANSFORMATION JOURNEY

When the Spirit of God began to invade my life, He came to a young teenager whose life had been defined by the darkness of fatherly abandonment, sexual abuse and poverty. In fact, these patterns marked not only my life but that of the generation before me. The assault of darkness against my family and me ultimately informed how I thought about myself and shaped the way I lived. Fatherlessness has a way of convincing you that you are insignificant and unimportant; no amount of encouragement or success can convince you otherwise. Sexual abuse can cover you in shame and set your life on a path of hiddenness and immorality. Poverty can forge a mindset that causes you to view life through reading lenses; only seeing what's right in front of you—unable to look further down the road, dream, or envision your life beyond what you've known. These voices of injustice gave definition to my identity, until Christ redefined me.

In my early teenage years, my mom stood in my bedroom the morning of a homecoming football game. She was startled by a dream she had the night before and urged me not to play in the football game that evening. I blew her off. She, however, picked up the phone and called her new church friends asking them to pray for me. She told them God came to her in a dream the night before and instructed her to pray that I would live and not die!

In the third quarter of the game I collapsed on the field. I remember vomiting and then having seizures. Finally, there were sirens; I blacked out. I was rushed to the hospital where I underwent 3.5 hours of emergency brain surgery due a blood clot on my brain sustained during the football game. I should have died on the field just as the young man in our county did the following year, due to the same injury. However, forewarned in a dream, my mom fell to her knees on the field and went to battle with the prayer God had given her. I am alive today because of God's mercy and my mom's intercession.

New Identity

The next two weeks my mom would sit on my recovery bed with an open Bible. When my mom read out loud the scriptures, the very presence of Jesus would fill the room. Each day as she read, Jesus would draw near and I wept as I was enveloped by His strong love. In those encounters the Holy Spirit was communicating Jesus to me (John 16:14). He was witnessing to me and leading me to the truth that *God is love* (1 John 4:8) and *I am loved by Him* (John 3:16). Weeks later I attended a dynamic youth ministry where I responded to the gospel with repentance and faith. I became an active member of that church where I was discipled in my early years with Christ and flourished as a young evangelist and preacher. However, in spite of the great leaders investing in me, significant holes remained in my spiritual life.

Like many kids who grow up fatherless, I fell into the trap of living for the praise of man. The gracious words of church leaders who wished to encourage my heart for God could not satisfy my insatiable need for affirmation and approval. No amount of encouragement nor achievement can shout louder than the voice of unhealed pain. The bottom line was that I didn't know who I was and I was leveraging all of my strength and gifting to earn a sense of value and identity. I was a walking identity crisis; unaware that God had already defined me.

My identity crisis came to a climax when I was 18 years old. My mom and I were in a heated conversation. Literally, we were screaming at each other. My mom yelled out, "What's really the issue here, Adam?!" I broke down in tears and in a moment of weakness shouted some honest words, "You never say you're proud of me, Mom!" The words of a young man who did not yet know who he was in Christ.

Later that night God would take initiative to end my identity crisis.

"The Lord, your Father, HE is proud of you, Adam. He is proud of you!" I can still hear the British accent speaking to me as I lay weeping on the conference floor in San Jose, CA in 2000, totally lost in the ecstasy of the Father's love. He continued, "Adam, even though your earthly father has been absent, the Lord wants you to know that He, your heavenly Father, has always been there . . . He loves you. Adam, He has been with you . . .Yes, He was with you on *sports day*, Adam. Your heavenly Father was there on *sports day.*" This man, who I had never met before, was speaking with incredible insight to the depths of my heart; I was undone.

God was shouting my identity: *You are a son of God!*

In one encounter, the Father drew near and gave me a small taste of what he declared over Jesus, *"This is my beloved Son, with whom I am well pleased."* (Matt. 3:17) I received God's word *about me.* I have been feeding on that truth ever since.

Now years later, I have grown into my sonship and my deepest areas of pain have become my deepest ministry. I am happy to celebrate that my four children are the first kids in several generations in my family who will grow up with Christ in from the beginning. They are the first generation who will have mom and dad married and together in the home. They are the first generation who will not know divorce, sexual abuse, poverty or fatherlessness.

How did this transformation happen?

Jesus showed me the Father. Daily I behold Him and He calls me His son. His words are life to me. His words have redefined me. I have been fathered well. As a result, I can be a husband and a father.

I embraced my new identity and discovered it was a supernatural key to unlock my purpose and calling.

TIPS FOR YOUR JOURNEY

Team up with friends.
Grab a friend or a few to take the *New Identity* journey with you. A team will see greater long-term transformation in their lives and community than an individual in isolation.

Make space in your schedule.
It's been said that if you fail to plan, you plan to fail. It's vital that you schedule time each day for your journey. Time will not tell you how to use it; it's a currency that will simply decrease as you spend it. Value your journey; budget time for it daily.

Go slow and complete each step each day.
It is possible to speed through each day. But you will see a greater reward if you move slowly and prayerfully, sensitive to God's presence and voice. A variety of devotional practices are prescribed throughout the journey. Some of them will be new to you. New things are not always comfortable; but when God is in them, they always produce good fruit.

Use the resources at the back of the book.
Do yourself a favor and check out the Glossary, 4-R Prayer Model and Spiritual Gift List. Get acquainted with the terms you'll find throughout the journey.

Talk to others about your New Identity journey.
Sharing about your journey with others will help you connect dots, apply what you are learning and retain the revelation God gives you. As well, you might encourage someone else to begin their own journey. Use the hashtag: **#NewIdentity**

Make a decision to finish what you start.
Plan to finish the journey no matter what. The Personal Identity Declaration on the final day is a powerful tool you don't want to miss.

DAY 1

I AM A NEW CREATION

I t was 2:00 a.m. and I was preparing Nina, our newborn, for a feeding. While Jenny was getting situated I leaned over the hospital bed and held Nina in my hands. I was half-awake and yet completely enamored. I couldn't take my eyes off her little face. Even in the midst of disorienting sleep deprivation and the intoxicating effects of my little girl's love spell, I could clearly understand one thing: the arrival of this new life would change everything.

The truth of the new creation reminds us each day that we are not defined by our past. We are now clean, pure, and innocent—little babes in the hands of the Father. We are not the sum total of our failures, sin and pain; we have been reborn and redefined by grace. This is not merely a second chance at life but an altogether, brand new life through the death and resurrection of Jesus. The truth of the new creation is the engine that drives spiritual transformation.

Even as my own eyes were fixed on my newborn, so the Father's eyes are fixed on you. He delights in you today and dreams of the person you are yet to become.

SCRIPTURES FOR MEDITATION

2 Corinthians 5:17

Therefore, if anyone is in Christ, he is a new creation. The old has passed away; behold, the new has come.

Galatians 2:20

I have been crucified with Christ. It is no longer I who live, but Christ who lives in me. And the life I now live in the flesh I live by faith in the Son of God, who loved me and gave Himself for me.

Ezekiel 36:26-27

And I will give you a new heart, and a new spirit I will put within you. And I will remove the heart of stone from your flesh and give you a heart of flesh. And I will put my Spirit within you, and cause you to walk in my statutes and be careful to obey my rules.

1 Corinthians 2:16

"For who has understood the mind of the Lord so as to instruct him?" But we have the mind of Christ.

PERSONAL REFLECTION

1. Embracing your identity as a new creation often involves confronting competing thoughts (lies) about yourself that challenge God's truth. List 2–5 thoughts about your past that compete with your new identity in Christ.

   1. _____

   2. _____

   3. _____

   4. _____

   5. _____

2. Write out Galatians 2:20. Replace the first two personal pronouns ("I") with your past sin from Question 1. This prayer declares that your past has been crucified with Christ.

3. Read Acts 9:1—31, the story of Saul's conversion. As you read, ask God to help you embrace your identity as a new creation with the same fierceness as Saul.

DECLARATION

In the name of Jesus, I declare that I am a new creation in Christ. The old me is dead, buried and gone. I am new. I was crucified with Jesus. I was buried with Him. My new life emerged with Him from the grave. I have a new mind to think the thoughts of Christ and a new heart to feel the emotions of Christ. My spirit is now alive in Him. I am new.

DAY 2

I AM RIGHTEOUS

The last time my wife took our kids school shopping my son, Gabriel, came home decked out head-to-toe in American patriotic wear. Everything he picked out was red, white and blue and covered with the American flag. To this day I don't know which of his friends at school influenced his brief stint with patriotic threads; but I do know this, for the next few months no one would have any reason to question Gabriel's nationality or patriotism—his clothes gave him away.

A glorious transaction has taken place in the spiritual realm—Christ has clothed us with His own righteousness! Our filthy rags of sin have been removed; from head to toe we have been clothed in Christ. We are not identified by our past or present struggle or even our ethnicity or nationality; we are identified by righteousness of Jesus. Our heart is now at rest as we stand before God righteous, secure and lacking nothing.

Before the Father there is no question about your status—your clothes give you away. You are righteous in Christ. This position of grace changes everything.

SCRIPTURES FOR MEDITATION

Romans 3:21—26

But now the righteousness of God has been manifested apart from the law, although the Law and the Prophets bear witness to it—the righteousness of God through faith in Jesus Christ for all who believe. For there is no distinction: for all have sinned and fall short of the glory of God, and are justified by His grace as a gift, through the redemption that is in Christ Jesus, whom God put forward as a propitiation by his blood, to be received by faith. This was to show God's righteousness, because in His divine forbearance He had passed over former sins. It was to show His righteousness at the present time, so that He might be just and the justifier of the one who has faith in Jesus.

Romans 5:17

For if, because of one man's trespass, death reigned through that one man, much more will those who receive the abundance of grace and the free gift of righteousness reign in life through the one man Jesus Christ.

2 Corinthians 5:21

For our sake He made him to be sin who knew no sin, so that in Him we might become the righteousness of God.

PERSONAL REFLECTION

1. Read Zechariah 3:1—5. This Old Testament passage is a dramatic picture that foreshadowed how God would clothe each of us with the righteousness of Christ. As you read, take notes below.

   A. What is the primary activity of Satan in this passage?

   B. What actions are attributed to God in this passage?

   C. What actions are attributed to Joshua, the High Priest, in this passage?

2. Living in the truth of our righteous identity promotes humility and grace toward others because we know we've done nothing to earn it. By contrast, criticism of others is a common symptom of self-righteousness. Take the spiritual inventory below and ask God to bring to mind any areas of your life out of alignment with the righteousness of Christ.

   Do I openly criticize people? Is my heart posture towards them bent towards blessing or criticism?
   • Spiritual leaders
   • Bosses
   • Co-workers
   • Family Members
   • Roommates
   • Other Churches/Ministries

3. Use the 4-R Prayer Model (Repent–Receive–Rebuke–Replace) to turn away from self-righteousness and criticism of others.

 # DECLARATION

In the name of Jesus, I declare that I am righteous. Jesus Christ, the Righteous One, who suffered, died and resurrected has given me His own righteousness. I do not stand in my own goodness or merit. I stand in Christ. I have access to the Father because I am clothed in the pure garments of Christ, my intercessor, whose blessing I receive as my own. I am righteous in Christ.

I AM ACCEPTED

A few years into my walk with Jesus I became aware of how much my heart desired the affirmation and praise of man. The generous encouragement I received from leaders in my church family felt incredible; it was life giving. However, I didn't understand that the attention, affirmation and praise of man was never designed to quench the God-shaped thirst of my heart for love and acceptance; it was only meant to compliment what I first received from God. This misdirected thirst would produce much internal turmoil for me, until I learned how to direct it to the only One who could satisfy.

The Father's acceptance of us through Christ quenches the God-designed thirst in our hearts for love and acceptance. Until this thirst is quenched by Christ, we will endlessly drink the praise of man in all of its forms. Likely, we will also continue in the pain caused by others' rejection of us. Our acceptance in Christ frees us from the addictive poison of the praise of man and brings healing to rejection's wounds.

Today, drink in the truth of your acceptance in Christ. May the Father flush out rejection's poison and establish you in His strong love.

SCRIPTURES FOR MEDITATION

John 6:37—40

"All that the Father gives me will come to me, and whoever comes to me I will never cast out. For I have come down from heaven, not to do my own will but the will of Him who sent me. And this is the will of Him who sent me, that I should lose nothing of all that He has given me, but raise it up on the last day. For this is the will of my Father, that everyone who looks on the Son and believes in him should have eternal life, and I will raise Him up on the last day."

Ephesians 1:3—6

Blessed be the God and Father of our Lord Jesus Christ, who has blessed us in Christ with every spiritual blessing in the heavenly places, even as he chose us in Him before the foundation of the world, that we should be holy and blameless before Him. In love he predestined us for adoption to Himself as sons through Jesus Christ, according to the purpose of his will, to the praise of His glorious grace, with which he has blessed us in the Beloved.

Ephesians 2:17—18

And He came and preached peace to you who were far off and peace to those who were near. For through Him we both have access in one Spirit to the Father.

PERSONAL REFLECTION

1. Healing from the pain of rejection begins when we present experiences of rejection before God with a heart to forgive those who have sinned against us. Ask God to bring to mind any people whose rejection of you still affects your thinking. Write their names below.

2. Pray a prayer of petition asking God for grace to forgive the names you listed above, even as Christ has forgiven you.

3. To the best of your ability today, declare forgiveness over each name above.

4. Pray for God's highest blessing to fall on each of the names listed (Luke 6:28). Blessing those who mistreat you is a supernatural weapon that can help you step into freedom!

5. Often our responses to rejection are aligned with sin rather than righteousness. Over time these responses can become normative and shape how we think and live in unhealthy ways. In order to eradicate the negative influence of rejection from our identity, we must identify and repent for our sin responses to rejection. Take the spiritual inventory below and ask God to bring to mind any areas where you are to realign to God's kingdom.

   A. Do I assume people don't like, care about, or have time for me (rejection mindset)?

   B. Do I struggle with taking initiative in establishing new friendships out of fear of rejection?

   C. Do I seek a sense of personal value from leaders in my life that only God can give?

   D. Do I strain friendships with unhealthy expectations?

6. Use the 4-R Prayer Model (Repent–Receive–Rebuke–
    Replace) to turn away from responses to rejection that you
    listed above.

 ## DECLARATION

In the name of Jesus, I declare that I am accepted by God. Though once separated and alone, I have been brought near through the blood of Jesus. God has sought me out, called me by name and identified me as His own. I stand in the light of God's approval of me. I refuse to live under the shadows of rejection in this life. My pain has been eclipsed by God's great love. I am accepted by God through Christ Jesus.

I AM GOD'S IMAGE BEARER

"I want to do this the rest of my life!" These were my exact words at the end of my first mission trip to Mexico as a high school student. I was covered in dirt from the field we camped in; I hadn't showered in a week; and I was hungry for a cheeseburger! But my heart was full. I had preached the gospel for the first time and had seen dozens surrender their lives to Christ. It was a glimpse of my future. That week God placed His finger on some of the things He put inside of me—He showed me a bit of how He had designed me to uniquely display His glory.

God has designed each human with unique capacity to reflect Him. Our strengths, talents, personalities and spiritual gifts are not by accident. They have been deposited into our lives by God; they find their highest expression in communicating something of God to the world around us. This is the original design Jesus came to restore us to: God's image bearer.

When we catch a vision for reflecting God's glory certain motivations work their way into our lives. First, we get motivated to identify how God has uniquely designed us—we want to know how we are uniquely made to bring Him glory. Second, we get motivated to develop our unique strengths in a way that maximizes His glory in our lives—we open ourselves to training and development. Third, we get motivated to reflect Christ's character and nature in our lives—we open ourselves to the transforming work of the Spirit because we are concerned not only about our gifting but about our character.

The image bearer identity shapes our lives from the inside out. Let God put His finger on you today and point out those unique aspects of your life that are designed to bring Him glory.

 ## SCRIPTURES FOR MEDITATION

Genesis 1:26—27

Then God said, "Let us make man in our image, after our likeness. And let them have dominion over the fish of the sea and over the birds of the heavens and over the livestock and over all the earth and over every creeping thing that creeps on the earth." So God created man in His own image, in the image of God he created him; male and female he created them.

Psalm 139:13—18

For you formed my inward parts; you knitted me together in my mother's womb. I praise you, for I am fearfully and wonderfully made. Wonderful are your works; my soul knows it very well. My frame was not hidden from you, when I was being made in secret, intricately woven in the depths of the earth. Your eyes saw my unformed substance; in your book were written, every one of them, the days that were formed for me, when as yet there was none of them. How precious to me are your thoughts, O God! How vast is the sum of them! If I would count them, they are more than the sand. I awake, and I am still with you.

Ephesians 2:10

For we are his workmanship, created in Christ Jesus for good works, which God prepared beforehand, that we should walk in them.

PERSONAL REFLECTION

1. Each person is made to reflect God's image and glory in a special and unique way.

   A. What aspects of your personality do you feel reflect something of God?

   B. What strengths do you carry? Consider what others have observed about you.

   C. What spiritual gifts do you see operating in your life? Consider how God has used you.

2. What belief or attitude do you feel most inhibits you from reflecting God's image and glory in your life?

3. Are there people in your life, presently or in your past, whose voices challenge the truth that you are fearfully and wonderfully made? If so, step into freedom by taking the below steps:

   A. Identify whose voice hinders you and write exactly what they said against you.
   B. Declare forgiveness to these people by name for what they've done (be specific).
   C. Ask for God's mercy and grace to flood their lives for His glory (Luke 6:28).
   D. In Christ's authority, rebuke any hindering words and command them out of your life in Jesus' name.

DECLARATION

In the name of Jesus, I declare that I am an image-bearer of God. God, the great creative, envisioned me and fashioned me according to His design. I am made to reflect His image and glory. My personality, gifts and wiring are unique and have capacity to put Him on display. I am most myself when I am aligned to Christ. I am most unique when I abide in Him. I am an image-bearer of God.

I AM A SHEEP WHO HEARS

"Owen . . . because his heart is hurting." This was my three-year old's (Elli) response to my out loud question in prayer, "Father, who is on your heart for us to pray for right now?" What Elli didn't know was that morning Owen had packed his belongings and began driving across the country without even saying goodbye. It was a bit impulsive as his girlfriend had just cut things off and in his pain, he quit everything and ran; he was devastated. As I rocked my little girl we prayed the prayer God gave us for our dear friend. I smiled at God as I thought about his intimate connection with Elli. She was just three years old and she was already hearing His voice.

The supernatural grace to hear the voice of God is given to every believer. This is not a special gift reserved for the spiritual elite. This is the inheritance of every Jesus-follower. You don't have to be a prophet to hear the voice of God; you just have to be a sheep!

When we embrace our identity as sheep of the Good Shepherd, we position our minds with an eager readiness and expectation to hear from God. This simple truth can release spectacular God experiences in our lives.

SCRIPTURES FOR MEDITATION

John 10:3a—5

The sheep hear His voice, and He calls His own sheep by name and leads them out. When He has brought out all His own, He goes before them, and the sheep follow Him, for they know His voice. A stranger they will not follow, but they will flee from him, for they do not know the voice of strangers.

John 10:27—28

My sheep hear my voice, and I know them, and they follow me. I give them eternal life, and they will never perish, and no one will snatch them out of my hand.

Matthew 4:4

But he answered, "It is written, "'Man shall not live by bread alone, but by every word that comes from the mouth of God.'"

PERSONAL REFLECTION

1. Jesus said His sheep would not follow the voice of a stranger. Review the list below of key differences between God's voice and the voice of the evil one:

GOD'S VOICE	SATAN'S VOICE
CALMS	OBSESSES
COMFORTS	WORRIES
CONVICTS	CONDEMNS
ENCOURAGES	DISCOURAGES
ENLIGHTENS	CONFUSES
LEADS	PUSHES
REASSURES	FRIGHTENS
STILLS	RUSHES

2. Circle 1-2 comparisons listed above that stand out to you in discerning the voice of God. Why are these meaningful to you right now?

3. Intercessory prayer (prayer for others) is one of the best practices for hearing God. Take the below steps to engage intercessory prayer.

   A. Ask God to show you who is on His heart for you to pray for right now. Write their name.
   B. Wait and listen for any specific sense on how to pray for them. Write what you receive.
   C. Ask God to move your heart with His heart for them. Write down anything you feel.
   D. Spend time praying for them based on what you received from God.

DECLARATION

In the name of Jesus, I declare that I am a sheep who hears the Shepherd's voice. My Heavenly Father has inclined my ear to His voice. I live by every revelation that comes from His lips. His words are life to me. His words guide, teach, and direct me. His voice aligns me to His kingdom. I know His voice; the voice of a stranger I will not follow. I am a sheep who hears the Shepherd's voice.

DAY 6

I AM MADE FOR GOOD WORKS

I am indebted to pastors and leaders who taught me as a teenager how to share the gospel with others. Their empowering influence in my life set me up to participate in God's gospel movement as a young person. As well, it gave me opportunity to discover my love and passion for evangelism. I learned early on that I feel most alive when I am actively sharing Christ with others. I didn't realize it at the time, but following this passion to make Jesus known would help me discern my future calling.

Every Christian is designed for exploits with God. Our deep longing for purpose and our desire to make eternal impact for the kingdom is a feature of God's handiwork. It's a sign that we have been made in the image of a missional God.

Own the truth that God made you for good works. When you do, you position your life to discover and fulfill the dynamic purposes God has prepared for you.

SCRIPTURES FOR MEDITATION

Ephesians 2:10

For we are His workmanship, created in Christ Jesus for good works, which God prepared beforehand, that we should walk in them.

Matthew 5:14—16

You are the light of the world. A city set on a hill cannot be hidden. Nor do people light a lamp and put it under a basket, but on a stand, and it gives light to all in the house. In the same way, let your light shine before others, so that they may see your good works and give glory to your Father who is in heaven.

1 Corinthians 12:4—11

Now there are varieties of gifts, but the same Spirit; and there are varieties of service, but the same Lord; and there are varieties of activities, but it is the same God who empowers them all in everyone. To each is given the manifestation of the Spirit for the common good. For to one is given through the Spirit the utterance of wisdom, and to another the utterance of knowledge according to the same Spirit, to another faith by the same Spirit, to another gifts of healing by the one Spirit, to another the working of miracles, to another prophecy, to another the ability to distinguish between spirits, to another various kinds of tongues, to another the interpretation of tongues. All these are empowered by one and the same Spirit, who apportions to each one individually as He wills.

PERSONAL REFLECTION

1. Look over the Gifts List at the back of the devotional. Write down the top three gifts you see most operative in your life.

2. Consider your schedule for the next few days. Ask God to highlight to you the best opportunities to exercise your gifts in order to bless others and glorify Jesus. Write down your God-ideas and purpose in your heart to carry out those assignments.

3. Spend time asking God for a fresh release of the power of the Holy Spirit in your life so that this week your good works give light to Jesus in a fresh and unique way.

DECLARATION

In the name of Jesus, I declare that I am made for good works which God has prepared for me to walk in. God has equipped me with unique gifts, talents, and abilities to put Him on display through acts of mercy, justice, and supernatural power. God has designed mission assignments for me to carry out; every day is an adventure serving Him. Today, I align my heart to His agenda. I listen for His voice. I look for ways to put Him on display. I am made for good works.

I AM THE BELOVED OF GOD

I'm convinced that the love of God is one of the most contested truths in our lives. The evil one works double time to challenge any notion that we are valuable and loved by God. He mounts accusations against the simple truth of the gospel: God so loved the world (John 3:16).

The evil one knows that our behavior, lifestyle and our calling(s) flow from our identity. He understands that if he can compromise our identity, he can compromise our purpose. As result, he is relentless and assaults our identity in every season of life.

To embrace your identity as the beloved of God is to embrace that you are chosen, desired, and deeply valued by God. This is the ultimate rebuttal to the adversary's case. When you are grounded in the Father's love, you honor the ultimate sacrifice of Jesus and spiritual strongholds begin to be uprooted; lies are replaced with truth at a systemic level.

May the Father open your eyes to His great love today; you are indeed His beloved.

SCRIPTURES FOR MEDITATION

Matthew 3:16—17

And when Jesus was baptized, immediately he went up from the water, and behold, the heavens were opened to him, and he saw the Spirit of God descending like a dove and coming to rest on him; and behold, a voice from heaven said, "This is my beloved Son, with whom I am well pleased."

Matthew 17: 5

He was still speaking when, behold, a bright cloud overshadowed them, and a voice from the cloud said, "This is my beloved Son, with whom I am well pleased; listen to him."

Rom 5:6—8

For while we were still weak, at the right time Christ died for the ungodly. For one will scarcely die for a righteous person— though perhaps for a good person one would dare even to die— but God shows His love for us in that while we were still sinners, Christ died for us.

Ephesians 3:14—19

For this reason I bow my knees before the Father, from whom every family in heaven and on earth is named, that according to the riches of His glory he may grant you to be strengthened with power through His Spirit in your inner being, so that Christ may dwell in your hearts through faith—that you, being rooted and grounded in love, may have strength to comprehend with all the saints what is the breadth and length and height and depth, and to know the love of Christ that surpasses knowledge, that you may be filled with all the fullness of God.

Song of Songs 7:10

I am my beloved's, and His desire is for me.

 # PERSONAL REFLECTION

1. Jesus received His identity from the Father at His baptism, prior to entering into public ministry. One of the ways of God is to inform our identity before He assigns our calling (mission). List 3-5 reasons you suppose it is vital for you to embrace your identity as the beloved of God before taking on significant/new mission assignments from God.

2. Jesus had an encounter late in His ministry (Matt. 17:5) in which the Father reaffirmed His identity as the Beloved Son. Affirmation can come through new experiences as well as reminders of prior experiences. Strengthen yourself in the Father's love by journaling about a few times God communicated His love to you in a personal way.

3. Spend time praying Paul's apostolic prayer from Ephesians 3:14—19 over your life. Pray it out loud several times. Wait in silence for an extended time and write down anything the Lord brings to mind in prayer and meditation.

 DECLARATION

In the name of Jesus, I declare that I am the beloved of God. I have been made the target of His affection. I've been labeled by love. He chose me. He pursues me. He has won my heart. Because of love, I am His and He is mine. I am the beloved of God.

DAY 8

I AM JUSTIFIED

All parents of young children agree: The Magic Eraser is a game changer. That product has supernatural ability to remove any mark or stain from our walls and furniture. I don't know what parents did before the days of the Magic Eraser. I would bet money that after they walked by their kids' third and fourth fresh mural they internally pondered the 'golden' years of singleness, prior to kids. No doubt, the Magic Eraser has made homes all over the world a happier place.

Often it feels as though our sin and failures are permanent marks against us. We walk through the halls of our lives and are continually reminded of our shortcomings. The evil one will pour gasoline on the sparks of our internal guilt until our minds are consumed by the flames of condemnation instead of holy conviction. Conviction is a work of the Spirit that helps us see the wrong we've done; condemnation is a work of the evil one that tells us we are defined by the wrong we've done.

You are not defined by the wrong you've done but by the good Christ has done. The marks against you have been erased; God has declared you innocent. You are justified. You have been invited into God's righteousness, peace and joy in the Holy Spirit!

SCRIPTURES FOR MEDITATION

Titus 3:4—7

But when the goodness and loving kindness of God our Savior appeared, He saved us, not because of works done by us in righteousness, but according to His own mercy, by the washing of regeneration and renewal of the Holy Spirit, whom He poured out on us richly through Jesus Christ our Savior, so that being justified by His grace we might become heirs according to the hope of eternal life.

Romans 5:1—2

Therefore, since we have been justified by faith, we have peace with God through our Lord Jesus Christ. Through Him, we have also obtained access by faith into this grace in which we stand, and we rejoice in hope of the glory of God.

Romans 5:18—21

Therefore, as one trespass led to condemnation for all men, so one act of righteousness leads to justification and life for all men. For as by the one man's disobedience the many were made sinners, so by the one man's obedience the many will be made righteous. Now the law came in to increase the trespass, but where sin increased, grace abounded all the more, so that, as sin reigned in death, grace also might reign through righteousness leading to eternal life through Jesus Christ our Lord.

Romans 8:1—2

There is therefore now no condemnation for those who are in

Christ Jesus. For the law of the Spirit of life has set you free in Christ Jesus from the law of sin and death.

 PERSONAL REFLECTION

1. 2 Corinthians 7:10 is a scripture that contrasts the nature of true conviction from the Holy Spirit and condemnation. Write the scripture out below.

2. Our justification is a decree of God that the evil one greatly contests. Read today's scriptures out loud in a posture of spiritual warfare and command any accusatory or condemning voice to be silenced in Jesus' name.

3. Ask God for a fresh release of grace in your life to overcome sin. Ask Him to release godly sorrow in your life; that you would have a godly hatred for sin and would be more sensitive to the Spirit of God within you.

DECLARATION

In the name of Jesus, I declare that I am justified. God has decreed my innocence in Christ. I am clean. I have peace with God through Jesus and no one can take that from me. I rebuke the accusation of the evil one against me—Jesus Christ is my justifier and my righteousness. I am secure in Him. I am justified.

DAY 9

I AM RECONCILED TO GOD

Any healthy marriage understands the beauty of reconciliation. These marriages have been through conflict and pain and have seen intimacy restored through forgiveness. Restored intimacy is often richer than what was previously experienced, especially if a period of emotional and physical separation ensued during conflict. I've been known to jokingly tell people that my wife and I have reconciled at least four times—we have four kids!

In the theological sense, reconciliation goes beyond settling differences and merely making peace. It is about restored friendship and intimacy. God has repurchased us and made us right so that we might enter into eternal friendship with Him. This was His dream all along. The intimacy that Adam and Eve abandoned in the garden is now available to us with even greater dimension through the indwelling Spirit.

This is the essence of reconciliation: God has made a way for us to enjoy intimate friendship with Him.

SCRIPTURES FOR MEDITATION

Romans 5:10–11

For if while we were enemies we were reconciled to God by the death of his Son, much more, now that we are reconciled, shall we be saved by His life? More than that, we also rejoice in God through our Lord Jesus Christ, through whom we have now received reconciliation.

2 Corinthians 5:18—19

All this is from God, who through Christ reconciled us to Himself and gave us the ministry of reconciliation; that is, in Christ God was reconciling the world to Himself, not counting their trespasses against them, and entrusting to us the message of reconciliation.

Colossians 1:19—20

For in Him all the fullness of God was pleased to dwell, and through Him to reconcile to Himself all things, whether on earth or in heaven, making peace by the blood of his cross.

PERSONAL REFLECTION

The below phrases from scripture represent the work God has done in order for us to be reconciled to Him. Slowly meditate on each truth and respond to God in thanksgiving and worship. Write down any thoughts or impressions that come to mind during your meditation.

- **Incarnation.** God became a man and entered into the world.
- **Atonement.** God paid the price for the sins of humanity through the death of Jesus.
- **Resurrection.** God raised Christ from the dead, conquering sin and death.
- **Ascension.** God raised Christ into heaven where He is seated in glory.
- **Pentecost.** God sent the Holy Spirit to accomplish His plan of redemption in the world.
- **Redemption.** God has repurchased us from the kingdom of darkness.
- **Justification.** God has declared us innocent before Him.
- **Imputed Righteousness.** God has clothed us in the righteousness of Jesus.
- **Reconciliation.** God has made a way for us to enjoy intimate friendship with Him.

DECLARATION

In the name of Jesus, I declare that I am reconciled to God. I live as a joyful recipient of all that God has done in Christ Jesus. I will live rehearsing in the work of Jesus on my behalf. I will lay hold of the full measure of intimacy with God that is available to me. I am reconciled to God.

DAY 10

I AM DEAD TO SIN

I have had the privilege of serving Christ in various former communist and socialist nations. I have walked through the "killing fields" of Cambodia, along the wall in east Berlin and through the "House of Terror" in Budapest. Each of these preserved sites are reminders of the horrible tyranny that previously ruled those lands. Those evil governments have been overthrown—their power is broken. The landmarks remain, but the people have been liberated and now have opportunity to choose their freedom each day.

In Christ we have died to sin—it is not to have power over us any longer. To be dead to sin means that we are not to be ruled by sin. Sin is no longer a lifestyle that defines or dominates us. For the Jesus-follower, sin's tyrannical government has been overthrown. Tyranny only presides over the living—and we have died to sin in Christ.

A day is coming when not only the power of sin's tyranny is broken but its very presence is eradicated—the return of Jesus. Until that time, we daily consider ourselves cut-off from the sin-oriented lifestyle that previously governed us. We are under a new rule—the law of the grace.

SCRIPTURES FOR MEDITATION

Galatians 2:20

I have been crucified with Christ. It is no longer I who live, but Christ who lives in me. And the life I now live in the flesh I live by faith in the Son of God, who loved me and gave Himself for me.

Romans 6:1—14

What shall we say then? Are we to continue in sin that grace may abound? By no means! How can we who died to sin still live in it? Do you not know that all of us who have been baptized into Christ Jesus were baptized into his death? We were buried therefore with Him by baptism into death, in order that, just as Christ was raised from the dead by the glory of the Father, we too might walk in newness of life.

For if we have been united with Him in a death like his, we shall certainly be united with Him in a resurrection like his. We know that our old self was crucified with Him in order that the body of sin might be brought to nothing, so that we would no longer be enslaved to sin. For one who has died has been set free from sin. Now if we have died with Christ, we believe that we will also live with Him. We know that Christ, being raised from the dead, will never die again; death no longer has dominion over Him. For the death He died, He died to sin, once for all, but the life He lives he lives to God. So you also must consider yourselves dead to sin and alive to God in Christ Jesus.

Let not sin therefore reign in your mortal body, to make you obey its passions. Do not present your members to sin as instruments for unrighteousness, but present yourselves to God as those who have been brought from death to life, and your members to God as instruments for righteousness. For sin will have no dominion over you, since you are not under law but under grace.

✏ PERSONAL REFLECTION

1. Write out the three commands Paul gives in the above scripture.

2. What do you believe Paul means by being dead to sin?

3. Make a list (long or short) finishing this sentence. In the name of Jesus, I declare that I am dead to:

DECLARATION

In the name of Jesus, I declare that I am dead to sin. I have been baptized into Christ—into His death. Jesus' death on the cross means death to my old life of sin. I have been hidden with Christ—my old life is gone. Jesus declared, "It is finished!" I am dead to sin.

DAY 11

I AM A SLAVE
TO RIGHTEOUSNESS

This identity statement is perhaps the most offensive to our minds. The idea of being a slave invokes thoughts of hostility, compulsion and drudgery. However, the Apostle Paul applies the word slave to the Jesus-follower and declares that our slavery to righteousness is a free gift that leads to life! God calls us slaves to righteousness; His use of this phrase is radically redefining. Grace changes everything.

In similar manner, Jesus said, "Take my yoke upon you for my yoke is easy and my burden is light." Jesus used the imagery of a yoke, a laboring tool used to tie oxen together for field work, to describe the kind of invitation we have been given. We have been invited to be yoked to Jesus. This means the movement and direction of our lives are to be tied to the movement and mission of Jesus in the world. When we align to Jesus in holiness and move with Him in mission we find true rest for our souls.

As you engage today's devotion, ask God to renew the way you think about your relationship to righteous and missional living. Ask God to awaken you to the beauty of holiness and the supreme joy of partnering with God in His mission in the world.

SCRIPTURES FOR MEDITATION

Romans 6:15—23

What then? Are we to sin because we are not under law but under grace? By no means! Do you not know that if you present your-selves to anyone as obedient slaves, you are slaves of the one whom you obey, either of sin, which leads to death, or of obedience, which leads to righteousness? But thanks be to God, that you who were once slaves of sin have become obedient from the heart to the standard of teaching to which you were committed, and, having been set free from sin, have become slaves of righteousness. I am speaking in human terms, because of your natural limitations. For just as you once presented your members as slaves to impurity and to lawlessness leading to more lawlessness, so now present your members as slaves to righteousness leading to sanctification. For when you were slaves of sin, you were free in regard to righteousness. But what fruit were you getting at that time from the things of which you are now ashamed? For the end of those things is death. But now that you have been set free from sin and have become slaves of God, the fruit you get leads to sanctification and its end, eternal life. For the wages of sin is death, but the free gift of God is eternal life in Christ Jesus our Lord.

Matthew 11:28—30

Come to me, all who labor and are heavy laden, and I will give you rest. Take my yoke upon you, and learn from me, for I am gentle and lowly in heart, and you will find rest for your souls. For my yoke is easy, and my burden is light.

Galatians 5:25

If we live by the Spirit, let us also keep in step with the Spirit.

PERSONAL REFLECTION

1. Paul teaches that embracing our identity as slaves of righteousness leads to sanctification (the process of becoming like Jesus), and that sanctification is fulfilled in eternal life—a free gift of God. In human terms, slavery to righteousness sounds like hard work, but from heaven's perspective it's a free gift that leads to life. Spend some time meditating on the idea that being a slave to righteousness is a free gift that leads to life. How does this impact your day-to-day walk in righteousness? Write down anything in particular God brings to mind.

2. Jesus invites us to receive His yoke—to be tied to His movement and mission in the world. He promised that by receiving His yoke we would find true rest. In the kingdom, rest is reserved for the one who labors with God. How does this idea impact the way you view mission and rest?

3. Write down 3-5 reasons you think it is important for a Jesus-follower to embrace the identity of a slave of righteousness.

DECLARATION

In the name of Jesus, I declare that I am a slave to righteousness. It is my pleasure to be connected to Christ; to live happy and holy. Today I yield to the Spirit of God within me. I yield to His leadership. I move with Him in loving the Father. I move with Him in loving others around me. I am made to keep in step with the Spirit of God. I am a slave to righteousness.

DAY 12

I AM A CHILD OF GOD

It seems that the more kids my wife and I have stacked up the more our short-term memory has faded. Four kids into our beautiful family, we are no longer surprised by the things we forget. We simply make provision in advance to help us remember. Digital reminders, email reminders, text reminders—we use the best technological resources to fill the gap of our weakness.

Similarly, the Father knows the weakness of our flesh. He is well acquainted with the tendency of the human heart to forget or wander from truth. As such He has commissioned the best resource of heaven, the person and work of the Holy Spirit, to remind us of the things He has declared (John 14:26). The Holy Spirit is our guide and will lead us to all truth (John 16:13).

The Holy Spirit is continually reminding you of and affirming you in your new identity as a child of God (Rom. 14:16). The Father is intent on you carrying this revelation in a personal way; His Spirit declares that you are one of God's kids and your spirit replies "Abba" (Daddy)! The Holy Spirit is the best reminder.

SCRIPTURES FOR MEDITATION

Matthew 6:9

Pray then like this: Our Father in heaven, hallowed be your name.

John 1:11–13

He came to His own, and His own people did not receive Him. But to all who did receive Him, who believed in His name, He gave the right to become children of God, who were born, not of blood nor of the will of the flesh nor of the will of man, but of God.

Romans 8:14—17

For all who are led by the Spirit of God are sons of God. For you did not receive the spirit of slavery to fall back into fear, but you have received the Spirit of adoption as sons, by whom we cry, "Abba! Father!" The Spirit Himself bears witness with our spirit that we are children of God, and if children, then heirs—heirs of God and fellow heirs with Christ, provided we suffer with Him in order that we may also be glorified with Him.

1 John 3:1—3

See what kind of love the Father has given to us, that we should be called children of God; and so we are. The reason why the world does not know us is that it did not know Him. Beloved, we are God's children now, and what we will be has not yet appeared; but we know that when He appears we shall be like Him, because we shall see Him as He is. And everyone who thus hopes in Him purifies Himself as He is pure.

PERSONAL REFLECTION

1. Write down at least five characteristics of a child of God from the above scriptures.

2. Take each of the characteristics that you wrote down and write out a one sentence prayer of thanksgiving or a prayer of petition for each characteristic to grow in your life (e.g., Father, thank you that you have given me the right to be a child of God—something not determined by the will of man but by the will of God.).

DECLARATION

In the name of Jesus, I declare that I am a child of God. I have received the spirit of adoption; I am a chosen member of God's family. My daddy loves me. I reject the lie that I'm illegitimate. The Father has chosen me. I've been born again into His family. The Holy Spirit communicates with my spirit and affirms my status as a favored one. I've been made a target of God's love and affection. I am a child of God.

I AM A CHILD OF ABRAHAM

'll never forget my first experience of Sunday School as a young boy after a sleep-over at my friends' house. I distinctly recall all the kids being led in a song called "Father Abraham". I remember thinking this is the Christian Hokey Pokey! I had no clue who Abraham was, but I did learn some good dance moves that day. Not until my adult life did I learn the spiritual significance of being a child of Abraham.

In the Old Testament God chose Abram (later, Abraham) and his descendants (the Jewish people) to be a vehicle of blessing to all nations. They were to be a living picture to the world what it looks like to live under the rule and reign of God. This unique privilege however contributed to a sense of racial superiority among Jews who believed they alone were sons of Abraham. Naturally, significant historical division followed.

Jesus came as a descendent of Abraham; the ultimate picture of a life under God's rule. Through His death and resurrection, Jesus abolished divisions of race, gender and cast. Because of Jesus, Abrahams descendants are now from every race, gender and social status.

Our new identity as children of Abraham is the great equalizer; it honors our differences without privileging one over another. It empowers us to display some of the most sacred dynamics of heaven on earth: equality and unity in diversity.

SCRIPTURES FOR MEDITATION

Galatians 3:7—9

Know then that it is those of faith who are the sons of Abraham. And the Scripture, foreseeing that God would justify the Gentiles by faith, preached the gospel beforehand to Abraham, saying, "In you shall all the nations be blessed." So then, those who are of faith are blessed along with Abraham, the man of faith.

Galatians 3:27—29

For as many of you as were baptized into Christ have put on Christ. There is neither Jew nor Greek, there is neither slave nor free, there is no male and female, for you are all one in Christ Jesus. And if you are Christ's, then you are Abraham's offspring, heirs according to promise.

Ephesians 2:11—18

Therefore remember that at one time you Gentiles in the flesh, called "the uncircumcision" by what is called the circumcision, which is made in the flesh by hands— remember that you were at that time separated from Christ, alienated from the commonwealth of Israel and strangers to the covenants of promise, having no hope and without God in the world. But now in Christ Jesus you who once were far off have been brought near by the blood of Christ. For he Himself is our peace, who has made us both one and has broken down in His flesh the dividing wall of hostility by abolishing the law of commandments expressed in ordinances, that He might create in Himself one new man in place of the two, so making peace, and might reconcile us both to God in one body through the cross, thereby killing the hostility. And He came and preached peace to you who were far off and peace to those who were near. For through Him we both have access In one Spirit to the Father.

 # PERSONAL REFLECTION

1. Galatians 3:27—29 tell us that our status in Christ comes before every other earthly designation. The children of Abraham are not to be privileged or divided by race, gender or cast. Consider for a moment how this truth of the gospel, if lived out consistently, would impact your church. Would anything have to change in order for your church to embody the unity and equality presented in this scripture? List your thoughts below.

2. Often, we are guilty of operating with hidden biases that contribute to unhealthy distinctions and even divisions in church life. Ask God to uncover any hidden mindsets that limit you to relating with a limited demographic of people rather than all people from a variety of socio-economic, racial and generational backgrounds.

3. Spend an extended time interceding for your local church as well as the Church (universal). Target your prayers that the truth of Galatians 3:27—29 would be embodied by the people of God and that the world would witness the truth of the gospel in our midst.

DECLARATION

In the name of Jesus, I declare that I am a child of Abraham. By faith in Christ, I have been grafted into Abraham's family. Jesus has torn down the wall of hostility between humanity. In Christ there is freedom to enjoy oneness with my brother and sister. The gospel has made a way for equality and true unity in diversity. I posture my heart to embody this truth of the gospel. I am a child of Abraham.

DAY 14

I AM A BONDSERVANT

In stark contrast to the ordinary slave, the bondservant willingly volunteered for their master's service. They were not moved by compulsion or violence. Bondservants were motivated by great love for their master; they trusted his goodness. As a sign of their commitment, bondservants were pierced through (in their ear) by their master. This piercing was a sign to all that they had willingly surrendered to their master's leadership.

Jesus is the ultimate bondservant. In love, He too was pierced through as He bore our sins on the cross. Jesus lived and died in loving obedience to the Father. He lived for the praise of the Father alone. When the disciples jockeyed for greatness, Jesus did not rebuke them; instead He showed them heaven's way into true greatness: servanthood.

This is the identity we inherit in Christ—we are bondservants. We have been pierced through by the Father's love. We have tasted His goodness and we have willingly surrendered to His leadership. When we embrace our bondservant identity, we embrace the path to true greatness.

SCRIPTURES FOR MEDITATION

Exodus 21:1—6

"Now these are the rules that you shall set before them. When you buy a Hebrew slave, he shall serve six years, and in the seventh he shall go out free, for nothing. If he comes in single, he shall go out single; if he comes in married, then his wife shall go out with him. If his master gives him a wife and she bears him sons or daughters, the wife and her children shall be her master's, and he shall go out alone. But if the slave plainly says, 'I love my master, my wife, and my children; I will not go out free,' then his master shall bring him to God, and he shall bring him to the door or the doorpost. And his master shall bore his ear through with an awl, and he shall be his slave forever."

Matthew 20:20—27

"Then the mother of the sons of Zebedee came up to him with her sons, and kneeling before him she asked him for something. And he said to her, "What do you want?" She said to him, "Say that these two sons of mine are to sit, one at your right hand and one at your left, in your kingdom." Jesus answered, "You do not know what you are asking. Are you able to drink the cup that I am to drink?" They said to him, "We are able." He said to them, "You will drink my cup, but to sit at my right hand and at my left is not mine to grant, but it is for those for whom it has been prepared by my Father." And when the ten heard it, they were indignant at the two brothers. But Jesus called them to Him and said, "You know that the rulers of the Gentiles lord it over them, and their great ones exercise authority over them. It shall not be so among you. But whoever would be great among you must be your servant, and whoever would be first among you must be your slave, even as the Son of Man came not to be served but to serve, and to give His life as a ransom for many."

Phil 2:5—8

Have this mind among yourselves, which is yours in Christ Jesus, who, though he was in the form of God, did not count equality with God a thing to be grasped, but emptied Himself, by taking the form of a servant, being born in the likeness of men. And being found in human form, He humbled Himself by becoming obedient to the point of death, even death on a cross.

PERSONAL REFLECTION

1. Bondservants are motivated by love. Write out a prayer asking God to grow you in love as your primary motivation for service and obedience.

2. Bondservants live to serve and advance others. Write out a prayer asking God to give you opportunities to exercise your gifts to serve and advance someone else. Write down any ideas God brings to mind.

3. Bondservants live to please God alone. Read Matthew 6:1—4 and write out a prayer asking God to align your heart to His ways.

 DECLARATION

In the name of Jesus, I declare that I am a bondservant of the Lord Jesus Christ. My Master is good, kind and generous. He has laid His life down for me and I lay my life down in return. I have been pierced through by my Master's love and I have pledged my allegiance to Jesus. I am pursuing greatness through humility and service. I find life when I give my life away. I am a bondservant of Christ.

I AM REDEEMED

The prophet Hosea had a difficult road. God called him to purchase a wife out of prostitution. Sometime after starting a family, Hosea's wife abandoned her family and returned to the sex industry. Heartbroken and devastated, Hosea continued to obey God and repurchased his wife out of sex slavery. This purchase is the essence of redemption, which means to be bought back; or repurchased.

Hosea's call was to embody God's message to His people, Israel. In effect God was saying "I have paid the great cost to redeem you—to rescue you from slavery in Egypt and yet you have wandered from Me. Still, I will redeem you and you will return to Me; you are mine."

The relationship with God that you enjoy today has come at a greater cost than the great plagues released against Egypt and the money Hosea paid to repurchase his wayward wife. God the Father spent the life of His only Son to purchase you out of darkness. He alone has taken extreme measure to see you returned to Him. Because of Jesus, you are the redeemed of the Lord.

SCRIPTURES FOR MEDITATION

Ephesians 1:7—10

In Him we have redemption through His blood, the forgiveness of our trespasses, according to the riches of His grace, which He lavished upon us, in all wisdom and insight making known to us the mystery of his will, according to His purpose, which He set forth in Christ as a plan for the fullness of time, to unite all things in Him, things in heaven and things on earth.

Colossians 1:13—14

He has delivered us from the domain of darkness and transferred us to the kingdom of his beloved Son, in whom we have redemption, the forgiveness of sins.

Romans 3:21—26

But now the righteousness of God has been manifested apart from the law, although the Law and the Prophets bear witness to it— the righteousness of God through faith in Jesus Christ for all who believe. For there is no distinction: for all have sinned and fall short of the glory of God, and are justified by His grace as a gift, through the redemption that is in Christ Jesus, whom God put forward as a propitiation by His blood, to be received by faith. This was to show God's righteousness, because in His divine forbearance He had passed over former sins. It was to show His righteousness at the present time, so that He might be just and the justifier of the one who has faith in Jesus.

PERSONAL REFLECTION

1. Spend time meditating on God's redemptive work through Christ. Ask God to bring illumination as you reflect. Write below 3-5 thoughts that come to mind about the cost Jesus paid.

2. To be repurchased means a transfer of ownership. The gospel is the work of the Father spending the Son to acquire humanity for Himself. From this vantage point, read the parables of the kingdom found in Matthew 13:44—46 that describe God's act of redemption.

DECLARATION

In the name of Jesus, I declare that I am redeemed. I've been repurchased by God. In love, the Father spent the Son and acquired me for Himself. The Father has placed a value on my life—the blood of Jesus. I am of extreme worth and value before God. Today I align my heart to the truth of redemption. I am redeemed.

DAY 16

I AM A ROYAL PRIEST

I quit my first job as a young teenager because "it got in the way of my relationship with Jesus." Really, I wanted to attend a Christian music festival and when my request for time off wasn't approved, I quit to attend the festival. At the time it felt like worship—I 'sacrificed' my job to the Lord. What I couldn't see was that there was a way to both worship Jesus with my whole heart and keep my job. I unnecessarily viewed my responsibility with work at odds with my spirituality.

In every season of life, we carry responsibilities that are less than desirable. At times they can seem to outnumber the things we enjoy and feel as though they prevent us from loving Jesus well. I have learned that when we embrace our identity as priests, we begin to view our entire lives as worship to the Lord, not just the songs we sing and the things we give up. When we engage the undesirable parts of life with our priestly identity, our emotional connection to God increases and those tasks become altars of worship and connect points for intimacy with God.

Lay hold of your identity as a royal priest. Present yourself to the Lord as an offering of worship today. Invite the Holy Spirit to enter every aspect of your day with His presence and help you to carry out your responsibilities as worship to God. Then your songs will be reflective of your life which you have oriented to fulfill the great commandment: to love God with everything.

SCRIPTURES FOR MEDITATION

Revelation 5:9—10

And they sang a new song, saying, "Worthy are you to take the scroll and to open its seals, for you were slain, and by your blood you ransomed people for God from every tribe and language and people and nation, and you have made them a kingdom and priests to our God, and they shall reign on the earth."

1 Peter 2:4–5

As you come to Him, a living stone rejected by men but in the sight of God chosen and precious, you yourselves like living stones are being built up as a spiritual house, to be a holy priesthood, to offer spiritual sacrifices acceptable to God through Jesus Christ.

1 Peter 2:9—10

But you are a chosen race, a royal priesthood, a holy nation, a people for his own possession, that you may proclaim the excellencies of Him who called you out of darkness into His marvelous light. Once you were not a people, but now you are God's people; once you had not received mercy, but now you have received mercy.

Romans 12:1

I appeal to you therefore, brothers, by the mercies of God, to present your bodies as a living sacrifice, holy and acceptable to God, which is your spiritual worship.

Colossians 3:17

And whatever you do, in word or deed, do everything in the name of the Lord Jesus, giving thanks to God the Father through Him.

PERSONAL REFLECTION

1. Write out a prayer in which you present yourself to the Lord as a priest. Declare that your whole life is an offering of worship to Him.

2. Make a list below of difficult or unpleasant tasks currently in front of you.

3. Spend a few minutes in prayer presenting each of these undesirable responsibilities to the Lord. Invite the Holy Spirit to enter every aspect of your day with His presence and to help you to carry out your responsibilities as worship to God.

DECLARATION

In the name of Jesus, I declare that I am a royal priest of God. I have been called to honor the presence of the Lord and to worship Him with my whole life. I carry a responsibility to declare His praise and to represent Him before the world. Even difficult and unpleasant responsibilities I make into offerings of worship to the Lord, for His glory. I am a priest of God.

DAY 17

I AM A TEMPLE OF THE HOLY SPIRIT

God's fire led Israel through the wilderness, burned on the temple's altar and later suspended over the heads of the 120 in the upper room at Pentecost. That same fire rests in the lives of each Jesus-follower today. As temples of God's Holy Spirit, God's fire not only empowers us for mission but also for holiness.

The Holy Spirit has a way of making us increasingly uncomfortable with sin. As we journey with Him, more and more we love what He loves and hate what He hates. He is a consuming fire. Jesus embodied the Holy Spirit's fire when He cleansed the Temple. Angered by the money changers' perversion of the Temple, Jesus overturned tables and chased out swindlers with a whip He made with His own hands. At times, our journey must mirror this kind of fire and zeal to see true restoration to God's design.

The New Testament assigns us the identity of temples of the Holy Spirit when it calls us into sexual purity and wholeness. Even as God provided fire from heaven in the Old Testament, He has made His fire available to us, to burn up any sexual history that has turned our temple away from God's design. God's fire is here to set us free of shame and restore us to live as holy dwelling places for God by the Spirit.

 # SCRIPTURES FOR MEDITATION

John 2:13—17

The Passover of the Jews was at hand, and Jesus went up to Jerusalem. In the temple He found those who were selling oxen and sheep and pigeons, and the money-changers sitting there. And making a whip of cords, He drove them all out of the temple, with the sheep and oxen. And He poured out the coins of the money-changers and overturned their tables. And He told those who sold the pigeons, "Take these things away; do not make my Father's house a house of trade." His disciples remembered that it was written, "Zeal for your house will consume me."

Hebrews 12:28—29

Therefore let us be grateful for receiving a kingdom that cannot be shaken, and thus let us offer to God acceptable worship, with reverence and awe, for our God is a consuming fire.

1 Corinthians 6:18—20

Flee from sexual immorality. Every other sin a person commits is outside the body, but the sexually immoral person sins against his own body. Or do you not know that your body is a temple of the Holy Spirit within you, whom you have from God? You are not your own, for you were bought with a price. So glorify God in your body.

Matthew 5:27—30

You have heard that it was said, 'You shall not commit adultery.' But I say to you that everyone who looks at a woman with lustful intent has already committed adultery with her in his heart. If your right eye causes you to sin, tear it out and throw it away. For it is better that you lose one of your members than that your whole body be thrown into hell. And if your right hand causes you to sin, cut it off and throw it away. For it is better that you lose one of your members than that your whole body go into hell.

PERSONAL REFLECTION

1. Are there areas of your sexuality (thoughts, practice, history, etc.) that do not align with God's design for your life? Rest knowing that specific confession of sin to God releases specific cleansing (1 John 1:9) in your life. Take time to confess any areas of sexual immorality that require cleansing in your life. By faith, declare your forgiveness through Christ.

2. God's remedy for the shame of sexual brokenness involves confession of sin one to another. The practice of confessing sin to other believers releases healing into our lives (Jas. 5:16). When we take the brave step of sharing with trusted leaders

or friends the things we've done, as well as the things done to us, we take what was in darkness and move it into the light; this is where God's healing and restoration take place. Do you sense a need to break free of shame? Make a point to practice confession with a trusted friend or leader. The Father is eager to restore you to His original design.

 # DECLARATION

In the name of Jesus, I declare that I am a temple of the Holy Spirit. I am made to host the presence of God in holiness. I take authority over the voice of shame that works against me through sexual sin. What I have done is cleansed. What has been done to me is cleansed. I am pure. I declare grace and courage in my life to practice confession one to another, that I may be healed. I am a temple of the Holy Spirit.

DAY 18

I AM MORE THAN A CONQUEROR

Years ago, I heard Loren Cunningham, founder of Youth With a Mission (YWAM), say that the secret to his joy was a lifestyle of thanksgiving. This man pioneered the largest missions organization in Church history. He was the first human to travel to every country and territory on earth—and he did so for the sake of the gospel! When I heard his answer to the question of joy, I was stunned; I guess I expected his secret to be more adventurous and radical.

I have come to believe that thanksgiving is one of the chief practices of those who reign in life with Christ. I'm also convinced that it is one of the most neglected spiritual practices. As a result, many Jesus-followers live with minimal joy and do not experience the abundant life Jesus came to bring.

Rise above joyless mediocrity and strive to give thanks in all circumstances. This is the will of God for you. A lifestyle of thanksgiving is a radical adventure; it produces supernatural joy. You are more than a conqueror!

SCRIPTURES FOR MEDITATION

Romans 8:33—39

Who shall bring any charge against God's elect? It is God who justifies. Who is to condemn? Christ Jesus is the one who died—more than that, who was raised—who is at the right hand of God, who indeed is interceding for us. Who shall separate us from the love of Christ? Shall tribulation, or distress, or persecution, or famine, or nakedness, or danger, or sword? As it is written,
"For your sake we are being killed all the day long;
we are regarded as sheep to be slaughtered."
No, in all these things we are more than conquerors through Him who loved us. For I am sure that neither death nor life, nor angels nor rulers, nor things present nor things to come, nor powers, nor height nor depth, nor anything else in all creation, will be able to separate us from the love of God in Christ Jesus our Lord.

Romans 5:17

For if, because of one man's trespass, death reigned through that one man, much more will those who receive the abundance of grace and the free gift of righteousness reign in life through the one man Jesus Christ.

1 Thessalonians 5:16—18

Rejoice always, pray without ceasing, give thanks in all circumstances; for this is the will of God in Christ Jesus for you.

PERSONAL REFLECTION

1. To practice thanksgiving is to remember what God has done and to celebrate it. Make a list of 21 reasons you are thankful to God.

2. Are you facing a difficulty, trial or suffering today? Write out a summary of your challenge below.

3. Practice rejoicing in your challenge. Write out a prayer of thanksgiving in which you celebrate the work of the Spirit to shape your character, release hope, and impart God's love through this challenge.

DECLARATION

In the name of Jesus, I declare that I am more than a conqueror through Christ. I am in Christ and Christ is in me; I have the victory. The Holy Spirit enables me to endure suffering, rejoice in trials, and overcome temptation. Grace sustains me. Grace upon grace! I am not a victim; I am victorious. I am more than a conqueror through Christ.

I AM AN AMBASSADOR OF CHRIST

Recently we sent a Catalyst ministry team to Europe. When we prayed for the team before they left, I told them that they were going as official representatives of Catalyst and that they had authority to represent us—our ministry, interests, etc., in my stead. In effect, I was sending them out as ambassadors.

An ambassador is the highest-ranking diplomat of a nation in a foreign land. They have been delegated authority to represent their nation and their head of state.

You are Christ's ambassador. You have received authority and power from God to represent the interests of Jesus' heavenly kingdom on earth. When you embrace this identity, you align your heart to God's agenda on earth: bringing heaven to earth (Matt. 6:10) and making disciples of nations (Matt. 28:18—20).

SCRIPTURES FOR MEDITATION

Matthew 6:10

Your kingdom come, your will be done, on earth as it is in heaven.

2 Corinthians 5:17–20

Therefore, if anyone is in Christ, he is a new creation. The old has passed away; behold, the new has come. All this is from God, who through Christ reconciled us to Himself and gave us the ministry of reconciliation; that is, in Christ God was reconciling the world to Himself, not counting their trespasses against them, and entrusting to us the message of reconciliation. Therefore, we are ambassadors for Christ, God making his appeal through us. We implore you on behalf of Christ, be reconciled to God.

Colossians 2:9—10

For in Him the whole fullness of deity dwells bodily, and you have been filled in Him, who is the head of all rule and authority.

Acts 1:8

But you will receive power when the Holy Spirit has come upon you, and you will be my witnesses in Jerusalem and in all Judea and Samaria, and to the end of the earth.

Matthew 28:18—20

And Jesus came and said to them, "All authority in heaven and on earth has been given to me. Go therefore and make disciples of all nations, baptizing them in the name of the Father and of the Son and of the Holy Spirit, teaching them to observe all that I have commanded you. And behold, I am with you always, to the end of the age."

PERSONAL REFLECTION

1. 2 Corinthians 5:19 tells us that God is busy reconciling the world to Himself through us! God uses people in His pursuit of humanity. Write out a few of the names of people who God used in His pursuit of you. What role did they play in your salvation story? Thank God for their influence in your life.

2. Ask God to bring to mind names and faces of people in your life whom He is pursuing for their salvation. Write their names below.

3. Spend time in intercessory prayer for their salvation. Take care to listen for God's voice as you are praying for them. Write down anything you hear.

4. Ask God to bring to mind any ways you can partner with Him in His pursuit of these individuals. Write down those God-ideas and purpose in your heart to take initiative with those assignments.

📢 DECLARATION

In the name of Jesus, I declare that I am an ambassador of Jesus Christ. I am made in Christ's image. I have received Christ's Spirit. I have been given Christ's mind. I have been filled with Christ's authority and power to represent Him and His kingship on earth, until He returns. I am the highest-ranking diplomat of heaven on earth. I am an ambassador of Christ.

DAY 20

I AM A BRANCH

While teaching in our School of Transformation some years ago, John Dawson (International President of YWAM) made a profound statement. As only he could, in his brilliant Kiwi accent he said, "Everyone here is the product of a moment of intimacy. God has woven a rule into the fabric of creation: life flows from intimacy. As it is with the natural order, so it is with our spiritual lives. Life flows out of intimacy with God."

John's comment echoes the words of Jesus who taught that all spiritual fruit comes from abiding in the vine of Christ.

The Holy Spirit has grafted us into the ultimate life source—the vine of Christ. There we remain, in the grace of God, growing in close friendship with Jesus. To enjoy this growing intimacy with God is to lay hold of the highest purpose for our salvation; this is the essence of abiding.

We are mere branches; yet it is our responsibility to abide.

SCRIPTURES FOR MEDITATION

John 15:1—6

"I am the true vine, and my Father is the vinedresser. Every branch in me that does not bear fruit He takes away, and every branch that does bear fruit He prunes, that it may bear more fruit. Already you are clean because of the word that I have spoken to you. Abide in me, and I in you. As the branch cannot bear fruit by itself, unless it abides in the vine, neither can you, unless you abide in me. I am the vine; you are the branches. Whoever abides in me and I in Him, He it is that bears much fruit, for apart from me you can do nothing. If anyone does not abide in me he is thrown away like a branch and withers; and the branches are gathered, thrown into the fire, and burned.

Galatians 5:22—24

But the fruit of the Spirit is love, joy, peace, patience, kindness, goodness, faithfulness, gentleness, self-control; against such things there is no law. And those who belong to Christ Jesus have crucified the flesh with its passions and desires.

Jude 20—21

But you, beloved, building yourselves up in your most holy faith and praying in the Holy Spirit, keep yourselves in the love of God, waiting for the mercy of our Lord Jesus Christ that leads to eternal life.

PERSONAL REFLECTION

1. Intimate friendship with God is the essence of abiding. Write a paragraph style prayer to God asking Him to increase your fascination and enjoyment of Christ.

2. The fruit of the Spirit listed in Galatians 5:22—23 are the distinguishing features of one who abides in Christ. Write out one-sentence prayers next to each virtue listed below. Trust that God will cause this fruit to grow in your life as you abide.

Love

Joy

Peace

Patience

Kindness

Goodness

Faithfulness

Gentleness

Self-control

3. Spend five minutes praying in the Spirit (either with prayer language or your native language) according to Jude 20—21.

DECLARATION

In the name of Jesus, I declare that I am a branch grafted into the vine of Christ. In mercy, God has connected me to Him through Christ. I am blessed to abide in Him. I am blessed to rest in His love, walk in His truth and live by His power. I will live from this place of connection to Christ; I will remain here; He is able to keep me. I am His. I am a branch, grafted into the vine of Christ.

DAY 21

I AM A CITIZEN OF HEAVEN

I have travelled to dozens of nations. I've spent weeks, even months, with mission teams overseas. Interestingly, our teams have never once needed to be reminded that we were mere visitors in a foreign land. On many occasions, our new international friends would tell us they could spot that we were foreigners a mile away—*we look like our home.* As well, on extended trips our craving for meals, comforts and familiarities from home often increase. *We long for our home.*

Citizenship marks us more deeply than we understand.

Heaven's citizens walk the earth today as pilgrims and sojourners—those en route to glory. They do not go with the flow of the world; their lives stand out and bear an unusual culture. While the world may chase possessions and prominence, heaven's citizens build their lives around the things that truly matter. Their heart's desire has been set on God's presence and the eternal pleasures from His right hand (Ps. 16:11). *They look like heaven.*

Generosity is one of the chief marks of heaven's citizens—they give freely, joyfully and without reservation. They extend their hand to the poor and they sow their seed into good soil so that the Lord of the harvest may have His reward. They give because they reflect the goodness and generosity of their homeland. They give joyfully because they are convinced of their glorious heavenly reward. *They long for heaven.*

Align your heart to your heavenly citizenship today. It will change both what you model as well as what motivates you.

SCRIPTURES FOR MEDITATION

Philippians 3:20—21

But our citizenship is in heaven, and from it we await a Savior, the Lord Jesus Christ, who will transform our lowly body to be like His glorious body, by the power that enables Him even to subject all things to Himself.

Matthew 6:19—21

"Do not lay up for yourselves treasures on earth, where moth and rust destroy and where thieves break in and steal, but lay up for yourselves treasures in heaven, where neither moth nor rust destroys and where thieves do not break in and steal. For where your treasure is, there your heart will be also.

2 Corinthians 9:8—11

The point is this: whoever sows sparingly will also reap sparingly, and whoever sows bountifully will also reap bountifully. Each one must give as he has decided in his heart, not reluctantly or under compulsion, for God loves a cheerful giver. And God is able to make all grace abound to you, so that having all sufficiency in all things at all times, you may abound in every good work. As it is written, "He has distributed freely, He has given to the poor; His righteousness endures forever." He who supplies seed to the sower and bread for food will supply and multiply your seed for sowing and increase the harvest of your righteousness.

You will be enriched in every way to be generous in every way, which through us will produce thanksgiving to God.

 PERSONAL REFLECTION

1. Pray a prayer of petition asking God to give you a fresh revelation of eternity. Take a moment to meditate on the scope of eternity compared to your natural lifetime on earth. Write down any thoughts from your meditation below.

2. Generosity goes beyond finances. It's a posture of life that shares one's time, energy, money and reputation to benefit others. Prayerfully answer the below questions regarding generosity.
   A. How can I more generously invest my time to benefit others this week?

   B. How can I more generously invest my money to benefit others this week?

   C. How can I more generously invest my reputation to benefit others this week?

DECLARATION

In the name of Jesus, I declare that I am a citizen of heaven. God has transferred me from darkness to the kingdom of His Son; I belong to a different age. I fix my eyes not on what is seen, but what is unseen; for what is seen is temporary, but what is unseen is eternal. I refuse to live for the temporal; I live for eternity. I refuse to build my life around the lesser, fleeting pleasures of this life; I am living for the eternal pleasures that come from God's right hand. I am a citizen of heaven.

I AM ADOPTED INTO GOD'S FAMILY

It's been said that adopted kids are more special to families than those naturally birthed. When one is adopted, their parents choose them; whereas with a natural birth, parents are stuck with what they are given!

You have been adopted. You have been chosen. You are wanted. You have received a new status: son or daughter.

God is so intent on you walking in this new identity as His chosen kid—He has given you the Spirit of adoption to convince you and continually remind you of your new identity. The Bible tells us this is the truth that pulls you out of slavery to fear.

SCRIPTURES FOR MEDITATION

Romans 8:14—17

For all who are led by the Spirit of God are sons of God. For you did not receive the spirit of slavery to fall back into fear, but you have received the Spirit of adoption as sons, by whom we cry, "Abba! Father!" The Spirit himself bears witness with our spirit that we are children of God, and if children, then heirs—heirs of God and fellow heirs with Christ, provided we suffer with Him in order that we may also be glorified with Him.

Galatians 4:4—7

But when the fullness of time had come, God sent forth his Son, born of woman, born under the law, to redeem those who were under the law, so that we might receive adoption as sons. And because you are sons, God has sent the Spirit of His Son into our hearts, crying, "Abba! Father!" So you are no longer a slave, but a son, and if a son, then an heir through God.

Psalm 27:10

For my father and my mother have forsaken me, but the LORD will take me in.

PERSONAL REFLECTION

1. In Romans 8, Paul contrasts the spirit of adoption as sons and daughters with the spirit of slavery that leads to fear. The spirit of adoption makes us sons and daughters and yet many Christians still live under the influence of the spirit of slavery that leads to fear. Using that contrast, complete the sentences below:

   • Sons & daughters listen for God's voice because...

   • Slaves listen for God's voice because...

   • Sons & daughters follow God's leadership even when it's difficult because...

   • Slaves follow God's leadership even when it's difficult because...

   • Sons & daughters are at peace and rest when...

   • Slaves are at peace and rest when...

2. Can you think of an additional contrasting statement? Write it below.

DECLARATION

In the name of Jesus, I declare that I am adopted into the family of God. Jesus, the only begotten of the Father, has made a way through His death and resurrection to welcome me into the Father's house. I am not merely a slave serving the Master's household, I am a favored child. My mind is being renewed so that I might live from this truth. I have been given the Spirit of adoption—the Holy Spirit convinces my spirit that I belong to God. In joyful agreement, my spirit cries, "Abba!" I am adopted into the family of God.

DAY 23

I AM THE FRAGRANCE OF CHRIST

It wasn't long after I pledged allegiance to Jesus that I had my first experience of rejection because of Him. Subsequently, one of my best friends no longer had a buddy who would ditch youth group with him to get high at the park across the street and he wasn't happy about it. I'll never forget the creative nature of the choice language he used when I turned down his final offer. I remember thinking in that moment, He is not rejecting me; he is rejecting Christ in me. I may be losing a friend but I am gaining Christ.

The fragrance of Christ identity helps us walk among others with a humble confidence and security that comes from God. When we are received by others, we take joy in the fact that Christ is received. When we are rejected, we do not crumble but remain steadfast and devoted to Jesus. They are rejecting Jesus.

The fragrance of Christ solicits a human response; it's never neutral.

Too often Jesus-followers are silenced in evangelism due to fear of rejection. Truth is, rejection is certain. We would do well to anticipate rejection and purpose in our hearts to share Christ anyway. Until we settle that issue, we will continue to live tethered to the thoughts and opinions of man. Refuse to be tethered to anyone but Christ!

 ## SCRIPTURES FOR MEDITATION

2 Corinthians 2:14—17

But thanks be to God, who in Christ always leads us in triumphal procession, and through us spreads the fragrance of the knowledge of Him everywhere. For we are the aroma of Christ to God among those who are being saved and among those who are perishing, to one a fragrance from death to death, to the other a fragrance from life to life. Who is sufficient for these things?

2 Corinthians 3:4—6

Such is the confidence that we have through Christ toward God. Not that we are sufficient in ourselves to claim anything as coming from us, but our sufficiency is from God, who has made us sufficient to be ministers of a new covenant, not of the letter but of the Spirit. For the letter kills, but the Spirit gives life.

Matthew 5:10—12

Blessed are those who are persecuted for righteousness' sake, for theirs is the kingdom of heaven. Blessed are you when others revile you and persecute you and utter all kinds of evil against you falsely on my account. Rejoice and be glad, for your reward is great in heaven, for so they persecuted the prophets who were before you.

PERSONAL REFLECTION

1. Does the fear of rejection keep you from initiating with others when God has moved your heart to initiate? Write down the last time fear of rejection inhibited you.

2. The Bible calls us to cast our anxieties on God, for He cares for us (1 Pet. 5:7). Use the Prayer Model (Repent–Receive–Rebuke–Replace) to deal with the fear of rejection related to sharing Christ with others.

DECLARATION

In the name of Jesus, I declare that I am the fragrance of Christ. I have been infused with the life of Jesus by His Holy Spirit. Everywhere I go the Spirit wants to put Christ on display through demonstrations of His love, truth and power. I do not live for the praise of man, but the praise of God. God will encounter others through me in tangible ways. Today, I am positioned to listen and obey the voice of God. I am the fragrance of Christ.

DAY 24

I AM THE LIGHT OF THE WORLD

In my high school years, a leader challenged me to pray about how I could demonstrate the love of God in practical ways. As I prayed on this question the idea came to me to hand out free lollipops in math class. This simple, childlike idea provided an unsuspecting opportunity to preach the gospel to a classmate—*it's free, just like the love of God for you. But you must receive it!* I never anticipated reading a comment from a classmate in my yearbook later that year who told me that God used a lollipop in math class to lead her to salvation!

Light does not need to be sophisticated; it simply needs to shine. Light is not self-serving; it draws attention to whatever it illuminates.

We have been designed to draw attention to the goodness of God. When we exercise our gifts in service of others for God's glory, onlookers are given a demonstration of the character and nature of God. Without this sense of divine mission our spirituality will bend inward and eventually be overcome by self-serving religious practices that do not reflect the glory of God.

Embrace your light of the world identity and put Christ on display today!

SCRIPTURES FOR MEDITATION

Matthew 5:14—16

"You are the light of the world. A city set on a hill cannot be hidden. Nor do people light a lamp and put it under a basket, but on a stand, and it gives light to all in the house. In the same way, let your light shine before others, so that they may see your good works and give glory to your Father who is in heaven.

Isaiah 60:1—2

Arise, shine, for your light has come, and the glory of the Lord has risen upon you. For behold, darkness shall cover the earth, and thick darkness the peoples; but the Lord will arise upon you, and His glory will be seen upon you.

Psalm 34:4—5

I sought the LORD, and He answered me and delivered me from all my fears. Those who look to Him are radiant, and their faces shall never be ashamed.

Philippians 2:14—16

Do all things without grumbling or disputing, that you may be blameless and innocent, children of God without blemish in the midst of a crooked and twisted generation, among whom you shine as lights in the world, holding fast to the word of life, so that in the day of Christ I may be proud that I did not run in vain or labor in vain.

PERSONAL REFLECTION

1. Ask God for a *divine appointment;* a special, God-ordained opportunity to put Christ on display today in service of others. Wait in stillness and listen for any creative ideas the Lord may give. Write down anything you receive.

2. Psalm 34 tells us that those who look to God are radiant. Joy marks the countenance of every true worshiper. This radiance is attractive to unbelievers; it disarms resistance and provokes interest. Take five minutes and worship. May the kingdom of God manifest on your life in righteousness, peace and joy in the Holy Spirit (Rom. 14:17).

DECLARATION

In the name of Jesus, I declare that I am the light of the world. Christ has given me His Spirit who burns brightly the light of Jesus through my life. Everywhere I go the light of God is present to overcome darkness and put Jesus on display. My co-missioning with God by the Spirit gives opportunity for people to experience Jesus in real and tangible ways. Today I position my life that others may see Christ. I am the light of the world.

DAY 25

I AM THE BRIDE OF CHRIST

The Bride of Christ identity is not a designation of gender. Rather, it is a statement of the quality of intimacy God, the bridegroom, has assigned to our union with Him. Neither is it a statement applied to an individual; it is a label shared by a people. In fact, it is more biblical to say that *we are* the bride of Christ.

True intimacy with God produces Christian community. The two realities must never be separated. How we relate to the Church, Jesus' bride, is often a direct reflection of the quality of our intimacy with Jesus. Where there is distance between us and the bride of Christ, there is distance from Christ Himself.

To embrace this identity is to recover a value for intimacy with God and God's people that goes beyond the status quo. For that reason, aligning to our Bride of Christ identity requires a heart check. We must identify and overcome any heart issues that keep us from pursuing authentic community. In stark contrast to our western cultural trends today, individualism and independence are not supreme values for the bride of Christ—we are made for community.

SCRIPTURES FOR MEDITATION

Revelation 19:6—10

Then I heard what seemed to be the voice of a great multitude, like the roar of many waters and like the sound of mighty peals of thunder, crying out, "Hallelujah! For the Lord our God the Almighty reigns. Let us rejoice and exult and give Him the glory, for the marriage of the Lamb has come, and his Bride has made herself ready; it was granted her to clothe herself with fine linen, bright and pure"—for the fine linen is the righteous deeds of the saints. And the angel said to me, "Write this: Blessed are those who are invited to the marriage supper of the Lamb." And he said to me, "These are the true words of God." Then I fell down at his feet to worship him, but he said to me, "You must not do that! I am a fellow servant with you and your brothers who hold to the testimony of Jesus. Worship God." For the testimony of Jesus is the spirit of prophecy.

Psalm 133:1—3

Behold, how good and pleasant it is when brothers dwell in unity! It is like the precious oil on the head, running down on the beard, on the beard of Aaron, running down on the collar of his robes! It is like the dew of Hermon, which falls on the mountains of Zion! For there the LORD has commanded the blessing, life forevermore.

Acts 2:42—47

And they devoted themselves to the apostles' teaching and the fellowship, to the breaking of bread and the prayers. And awe came upon every soul, and many wonders and signs were being done through the apostles. And all who believed were together and had all things in common. And they were selling their possessions and belongings and distributing the proceeds to all, as any had need. And day by day, attending the temple together and breaking bread in their homes, they received their food with glad and generous hearts, praising God and having favor with all the people. And the Lord added to their number day by day those who were being saved.

PERSONAL REFLECTION

1. Ask God to increase your love for His bride, the Church. Ask Him to remove anything in your heart that hinders you from operating in God-quality love for his bride.
2. Take the below spiritual inventory on the topic of your heart towards the Church.
    A. Do I distance myself from Christian community due to church pain? (Yes / No)
    B. Do I distance myself from Christian community due to church disappointment? (Yes / No)
    C. Do I distance myself from Christian community due to church offense? (Yes / No)

3. If you've answered Yes to any of the above questions, it is vital that you release forgiveness to those connected to your answers. Freedom comes when you forgive; this is where God's healing begins to work in our lives. Ask for God's grace to forgive and declare forgiveness to these people.

4. When we forgive others, our capacity to love increases. Love takes steps towards others. Ask God to show you how you can take steps into greater intimacy with Him and others. Write down anything He brings to mind below.

5. Write out the apostolic prayer in Philippians 1:9—10 below and pray it over your own life in relation to Christ and His bride, the Church. Write down any insights to your meditation below.

 ## DECLARATION

In the name of Jesus, I declare that I am the bride of Christ. The Spirit introduced me to the bridegroom, gave me His righteousness and is preparing me for His return. I stand with the Church throughout the ages as the beloved of God. I do not stand alone. I am made for intimacy with God and Christian community. I will cultivate love for God and His people all the days of my life. I am the bride of Christ.

DAY 26

I AM A CO-HEIR
WITH CHRIST

The year 2007 was one of profound difficulty and pain for my wife and I. Never before in our ministry lives had we endured the compounding fires of public injustice, significant loss and physical suffering. In that sense, it was a season I wouldn't wish on my worst enemy. Ironically, it was also a year of unprecedented intimacy with God, rich with His presence, revelation and anointing. It was a year vital to my calling and destiny. In that sense, it was a season I hope for each of my friends.

At the end of that fiery season a friend shared with me that "God never wastes a good trial." That statement encapsulated my experience throughout 2007. By the grace of God, the intense pain and darkness of that year drove me daily into the presence of Jesus. As a result, I touched something of God's heart that was not previously available to me outside of suffering. I can look back on that year and say that I shared in the sufferings and the glory of Christ.

Our co-heir with Christ identity tells us that we are joint recipients with Jesus of all the heavenly blessings. But it is crucial that our framework for 'heavenly blessings' includes suffering as well as glory. This shouldn't cause us to adopt a fatalistic or pessimistic view of spirituality. Instead it ought to empower us to leverage even the darkest seasons of our lives to throw us further into God's glorious presence and heavenly purpose.

SCRIPTURES FOR MEDITATION

Romans 8:14—17

For all who are led by the Spirit of God are sons of God. For you did not receive the spirit of slavery to fall back into fear, but you have received the Spirit of adoption as sons, by whom we cry, "Abba! Father!" The Spirit Himself bears witness with our spirit that we are children of God, and if children, then heirs—heirs of God and fellow heirs with Christ, provided we suffer with Him in order that we may also be glorified with him.

Ephesians 1:3—6

Blessed be the God and Father of our Lord Jesus Christ, who has blessed us in Christ with every spiritual blessing in the heavenly places, even as he chose us in him before the foundation of the world, that we should be holy and blameless before him. In love he predestined us for adoption to Himself as sons through Jesus Christ, according to the purpose of His will, to the praise of His glorious grace, with which He has blessed us in the Beloved.

Philippians 3:7–10

But whatever gain I had, I counted as loss for the sake of Christ. Indeed, I count everything as loss because of the surpassing worth of knowing Christ Jesus my Lord. For His sake I have suffered the loss of all things and count them as rubbish, in order that I may gain Christ and be found in Him, not having a righteousness of my own that comes from the law, but that which comes through faith in Christ, the righteousness from God that depends on faith— that I may know Him and the power of His resurrection, and may share His sufferings, becoming like Him in His death, that by any means possible I may attain the resurrection from the dead.

PERSONAL REFLECTION

1. Sharing in the sufferings of Christ is not limited to religious persecution. In fact, when a Christian endures suffering of any kind and leans into Christ in the midst of it, their suffering becomes a pathway for greater connection with God. To suffer with Christ is to endure loss, rejection, hurt, and injustice from a place of righteousness and intimacy with God. What have been the top three greatest sufferings you've endured in your history with Christ? Write them below.

2. Suffering immediately becomes redemptive when we allow it to drive us into God's presence. Sadly, too many believers allow suffering to drive them away from God's presence. Write out a prayer dedicating your life to the presence of Jesus. Ask Him for grace to run into Him in the midst of difficulty and loss. Declare the truth of Jesus' victory.

DECLARATION

In the name of Jesus, I declare that I am a co-heir with Christ. Because of Jesus' substitutionary death and victorious resurrection and ascension, I have a new status. I am raised with Christ. I am honored before God as a joint-recipient of all the blessings in the heavenly places. I am no longer alone; I am joined to the family of God. I live in Christ, suffer with Him and will be glorified with Him at His return. I am a co-heir with Christ.

DAY 27

I AM SEALED BY THE HOLY SPIRIT

This identity statement can secure us in confident trust in the faithfulness of God. We have received a guarantee from God: the transformative work He began in us will be brought to completion at His return. This is what it means to be sealed by the Holy Spirit.

Accepting God's declaration that we are sealed by the Spirit can kill striving and religious performance. Our fear-based striving is often rooted in the lie that we must get better or else we will be rejected by God. The truth of the gospel straightens this crooked thought. The Father has given us His Spirit as a guarantee that we might be prepared and ready at the day of Christ.

This truth is not to settle us into passive resignation, leaving everything for God to magically do for us. Instead it ought to inspire and motivate us to faithful obedience and partnership with God. It provides assurance that we are not alone in our sanctification; God Himself is working in us to be conformed to the image of Christ. This transformation journey requires our participation, our obedience and our work. But our work is made effective by the powerful working of God in us!

God is faithful; He will do it—*with us*.

SCRIPTURES FOR MEDITATION

Ephesians 1:13—14

In Him you also, when you heard the word of truth, the gospel of your salvation, and believed in Him, were sealed with the promised Holy Spirit, who is the guarantee of our inheritance until we acquire possession of it, to the praise of His glory.

Ephesians 4:30

And do not grieve the Holy Spirit of God, by whom you were sealed for the day of redemption.

Philippians 1:6

And I am sure of this, that He who began a good work in you will bring it to completion at the day of Jesus Christ.

Philippians 2:12—13

Therefore, my beloved, as you have always obeyed, so now, not only as in my presence but much more in my absence, work out your own salvation with fear and trembling, for it is God who works in you, both to will and to work for His good pleasure.

Hebrews 12:1—3

Therefore, since we are surrounded by so great a cloud of witnesses, let us also lay aside every weight, and sin which clings so closely, and let us run with endurance the race that is set before us, looking to Jesus, the founder and perfecter of our faith, who for the joy that was set before Him endured the cross, despising the shame, and is seated at the right hand of the throne of God.

 # PERSONAL REFLECTION

1. Religious performance is antithetical to our sealed by the Holy Spirit identity. Religious performance can manifest in a variety of ways. Take the below spiritual inventory. Afterwards use the 4-R Prayer Model (Repent–Receive–Rebuke–Replace) to deal with any religious performance the Lord uncovers.

   > Do I represent my spirituality to others as though it is further along than reality?

   > Do I internally compete with other Christians around me in areas of spirituality?

   > Do I withhold information from others so they won't think less of me?

   > Do I struggle with letting others see my weaknesses?

   > Do I resist confessing my sins to others?

   > Do I find myself living for the praise or attention of others?

2. Ask God for the release of the Holy Spirit in your life in greater measure. Ask for supernatural assurance that He is with you and has sealed you for His glory. Wait in stillness before God and invite Him to minister to you in a personal way. Write down anything you sense from God.

DECLARATION

In the name of Jesus, I declare that I am sealed by the Holy Spirit. The Father has given me His Spirit as a guarantee of glory when Jesus returns. I rest in the truth that what God began in me He is able to complete for His glory. I lay down religious performance and I step into the bliss of honest transparency before God and others. I will not hide my weaknesses, but rejoice in the strength that God provides. I am sealed by the Holy Spirit.

DAY 28

I AM A CHILD OF
THE RESURRECTION

he most embarrassing moment I've had praying for others was with a restaurant server who was working with a severely injured foot. My embarrassment wasn't due to him not getting healed (he didn't get healed); it was due to the fact that I initiated prayer for his healing while I too had an injured leg. At the time I was in a boot and on crutches with a broken ankle! I'll never forget his face when I told him that I believed Jesus was alive and healed today.

No doubt my embarrassment in that restaurant got the best of me that day. But I refused to let it grow into hopelessness, stealing my expectation for seeing God's goodness break in. I know hopelessness can eventuate in abdicating my authority and no longer stepping out in faith. In fact, the following week I initiated prayer for my neighbor who needed a hip replacement (while I was still on crutches). Days later that neighbor ran out to greet me in the street with a wild report: he no longer needed a hip replacement; he had been healed! That man began attending church that week, gave his life to Christ and later became a deacon in his congregation.

The child of the resurrection identity reminds us that we belong to another age. We are destined for glory—a day when Christ returns and

His rule is in full effect. In that day all sin and sickness will be overthrown. Even death dies as we are all resurrected in glory. Until *that time*, we live to see His kingdom come and His will done on earth as in heaven. No one gets to decide how much of heaven is available to us today. For that reason, we never allow discouragement to keep us from taking risks and walking in faith to see God show up in others' lives with His love, truth and power.

 ## SCRIPTURES FOR MEDITATION

Luke 20:34—36

And Jesus said to them, "The sons of this age marry and are given in marriage, but those who are considered worthy to attain to that age and to the resurrection from the dead neither marry nor are given in marriage, for they cannot die anymore, because they are equal to angels and are sons of God, being sons of the resurrection."

1 Corinthians 15:24—26; 51—57

Then comes the end, when He delivers the kingdom to God the Father after destroying every rule and every authority and power. For He must reign until He has put all His enemies under His feet. The last enemy to be destroyed is death.
Behold! I tell you a mystery. We shall not all sleep, but we shall all be changed, in a moment, in the twinkling of an eye, at the last trumpet. For the trumpet will sound, and the dead will be raised imperishable, and we shall be changed. For this perishable body must put on the imperishable, and this mortal body must put on immortality. When the perishable puts on the imperishable, and the mortal puts on immortality, then shall come to pass the saying that is written: "Death is swallowed up in victory. O death, where is your victory? O death, where is your

sting?" The sting of death is sin, and the power of sin is the law. But thanks be to God, who gives us the victory through our Lord Jesus Christ.

 # PERSONAL REFLECTION

1. While the kingdom of God is present today and salvation, healing and deliverance are available in Christ, we long for the day when there will be no more death, disease or demonic oppression. This is the *groan* that is referred to in Romans 8:23. Write down 1—3 ways have you experienced this inward groan related to salvation, healing and deliverance.

2. Ask God to search your heart for any disappointment over not seeing breakthrough in seeing the kingdom come. Relinquish any disappointment to God and ask Him to renew your heart with true kingdom hope.
3. Ask God for fresh zeal to see a greater measure of the kingdom released through your life in salvation, healing and deliverance.

DECLARATION

In the name of Jesus, I declare that I am a child of the resurrection. I have been sealed by the Holy Spirit and I am longing for the return of Jesus when death, sin and evil will be defeated in entirety. Until then, I press in with faith. I believe for a greater measure of the kingdom released in my life in salvation, healing and deliverance. I am a child of the resurrection.

DAY 29

I AM BEING SANCTIFIED

At the time of this writing my wife and I have been married nearly 15 years. Often, when we are on a date we reflect on our journey together. We reference funny memories, tease each other about silly things we've done and delight in our children—we delight in our kids a lot. In essence, we take time to celebrate our journey. It's always fun to read the history we've written together; it's a practice that cultivates our intimacy.

I have found that my journey with Jesus needs its own reflection and celebration. When I view my life with God as a journey instead of a fixed destination, I am able to see transformation as a process rather than an event. Reading my transformation history with Jesus always leads me to thanksgiving and worship; it's a practice that cultivates intimacy.

From the moment of your salvation until the day of its completion at Jesus' return, you are being transformed to be more like Jesus. Sin patterns are being crushed, attitudes checked and heart motives purified—you are aligning to the character and nature of God within you. This process is an honor and privilege. This is the history you have with Christ: You are being sanctified.

Read your history with Jesus today. Honor and celebrate His work within you and let worship rise from your heart to the throne of God.

SCRIPTURES FOR MEDITATION

Romans 8:28—30

And we know that for those who love God all things work together for good, for those who are called according to His purpose. For those whom he foreknew he also predestined to be conformed to the image of His Son, in order that He might be the firstborn among many brothers. And those whom He predestined He also called, and those whom He called He also justified, and those whom He justified He also glorified.

2 Corinthians 3:16—18

But when one turns to the Lord, the veil is removed. Now the Lord is the Spirit, and where the Spirit of the Lord is, there is freedom. And we all, with unveiled face, beholding the glory of the Lord, are being transformed into the same image from one degree of glory to another. For this comes from the Lord who is the Spirit.

Hebrews 10:14

For by a single offering He has perfected for all time those who are being sanctified.

2 Timothy 3:16—17

All Scripture is breathed out by God and profitable for teaching, for reproof, for correction, and for training in righteousness, that the man of God may be complete, equipped for every good work.

PERSONAL REFLECTION

1. Sanctification involves change. God is shaping our lives to align to our heavenly identity. Take a moment to consider how God has been shaping you in the last month of Transforming Prayer devotionals. Complete the below sentences.
   In this month of Transforming Prayer devotionals:

   A. God has taught me the following about my identity…

   B. God has reproved (exposed wrong) me in the following areas…

   C. God has corrected (aligned to truth) me in the following areas…

   D. God has been training me in…

2. Write a prayer of thanksgiving to the Lord for His work of transformation in your life.

DECLARATION

In the name of Jesus, I declare that I am being sanctified. God has given me a heavenly identity and He is shaping my life to align to His design for me. My eyes are fixed on Christ and I am moving from glory to glory by the power of the Spirit. I embrace a lifestyle of joyful repentance and long for Christ to be formed in me. I am being sanctified.

PERSONAL
IDENTITY DECLARATION

Take time to answer the below questions—your answers will help inform your Personal Identity Declaration.

1. List 1—2 injustices (painful/unfair experiences) that have shaped the way you think, behave and live. If you have trouble identifying injustice in your life, ask God to help you see where you have been wrongly treated, experienced loss or shame. You may also refer to your answers to the Reflection Questions on I am Accepted and I am God's Image Bearer.

2. List 2—3 ways you responded to these injustices in an ungodly manner.
   For example, *I refused to forgive; I began hiding from others; I let anger/bitterness enter.*

3. List 1—2 sin patterns that have marked your family
   for generations.
   For example, *Criticalness; rebellion against authority; material-
   ism—living for the temporal; etc.*

4. List 2—3 lies you've believed about your identity and self-
   worth.
   For example, *Inferior; insignificant; damaged goods.*

5. List 2—3 negative thoughts you've struggled with about
   your future.

6. List 1—2 core lies God has shown that you previously
   believed about His character & nature.

New Identity

7. List 1—3 identity statements from your devotional that most reflect the opposite of the answers you listed above or most spoke to you.

8. Write down any memorable words of encouragement or prophecy that others have given you regarding your original design or spiritual identity.

9. List 1—3 spiritual gifts you've seen operative in your life.

10. List 1—3 truths of God's character that have been most significant to you.

PERSONAL IDENTITY DECLARATION TEMPLATE

Fill in the blanks below.

- **In the name of Jesus, I declare that I am** (insert your favorite identity statements).

- **My life is not defined by** (insert one-word titles to your answers from #1). **I am defined by the perfect work of Jesus Christ.**

- **I reject the lie(s) that I am** (insert your answers from #4).

- **The Father has** (insert what God has done for you with respect to this identity point).

- **I know what God has done; I know who I am.**

- (Insert answers from #2) **will no longer mark me. My life is being transformed by the power of Jesus' blood and resurrection.**

- **The shadows of** (Insert one-word titles to your answers from #3) **no longer have place in my life. I have died to sin; I live to Christ—I am alive.**

- **God has gifted me with** (insert list of spiritual gifts from #9) **for His glory. I live for the kingdom of heaven. My life is not my own; I belong to Christ. I carry eternal purpose.**

- **I'm convinced of the goodness of God—my future is blessed!**

- **I will live to** (Insert your own paraphrase of the command in Matthew 22:37).

- **It is my joy to** (Insert your own paraphrase of 2 Corinthians 3:18).

- **I receive power from the Holy Spirit to** (insert your own paraphrase of Matthew 28:18-19).

- **I will build my life on the character and nature of God. He is** (Insert your answers to #10).

- **This is my declaration.**

GLOSSARY

4-R PRAYER MODEL
A prayer model for repentance and spiritual strongholds.

ADORATION/WORSHIP
Honoring, celebrating and adoring God for who He is (John 4:23—24).

CONFESSION
Telling God or others about an area of sin in us (1 John 1:9; Jas. 5:17).

IDENTITY
Who a person is and the qualities that define them (Matt. 3:17).

INTERCESSION
Praying for others under the direction of the Holy Spirit (Rom. 8:26–28).

LISTENING PRAYER
Waiting in silence to hear God's voice in prayer (John 10:27).

MEDITATE
The practice of pondering while one's heart and mind are receptive to the Holy Spirit. Often Bible meditation is practiced using these five actions: 1-Read it. 2-Say it. 3-Write it. 4-Pray it. 5-Sing it.

ORIGINAL DESIGN
Each human is designed to display God's glory in a unique way (Eph. 2:10).

PETITION
Asking God for something we desire (Phil. 4:6).

REPENTANCE
Turning away from sinful mindsets and behaviors to God's ways (Rom. 2:4).

SPIRITUAL GIFTS
Supernatural abilities to glorify God by serving others (1 Cor. 12:4—7).

SPIRITUAL INVENTORY
Inviting God's Spirit to search our heart for spiritual renewal (Ps. 139:23—24).

SPIRITUAL STRONGHOLDS
Engrained mindsets and behaviors rooted in spiritual realties that challenge God's truth (2 Cor. 10:3—5).

THANKSGIVING
Thanking God for what He has done (1 Thess. 5:16—18).

THE 4-R PRAYER MODEL

A model for praying repentance.[1]

1. Repent of the sin.

Call it what it is. It is your sin. It may be a heart attitude like bitterness, rebellion, or pride. It could be a behavior, like alcohol abuse, immorality, or stealing. It could even be a feeling, like rejection, inferiority, or shame. (Note: In the instance of abuse of wounding, the initial sin is not your fault. Your sin is your response: anger, fear, unforgiveness, bitterness, shame, etc. Recognize the sin and confess it!)

Acts 3:19 (NIV) Repent, then and turn to God, so that your sins may be wiped out, that times of refreshing may come from the Lord.

2. Receive God's forgiveness and cleansing.

Ask God to fill you anew with His Holy Spirit; to strengthen you in your thoughts, behavior, and emotions.

Psalm 103:8—12 (NIV) The LORD is compassionate and gracious, slow to anger, abounding in love. He will not always accuse, nor will He harbor His anger forever; He does not treat us as our sins deserve or repay us according to our iniquities. For as high as the heavens are above the earth, so great is His love for those who fear Him; as far as the east is from the west, so far has He removed our transgressions from us.

1 John 1:9 (NIV) If we confess our sins, He is faithful and just and will forgive us our sins and purify us from all unrighteousness.

1   The Freedom Class Manual, Brian Brennt & Mike Riches 2007

3. Rebuke the enemy's hold on you because of sin.

Take your rightful place of authority through the power of Jesus' death and resurrection and renounce any comfort or "payoff" received from this sin.

Matthew 4:10 (NIV) Jesus said to him, "Away from me, Satan!"

James 4:7 (NIV) Submit yourselves, then, to God. Resist the devil, and he will flee from you.

4. Replace all lies with God's TRUTH!

Declare old attitudes, actions, and emotions dead and "paid for." Fill your heart and mind with TRUTH that is consistent with the character of Jesus Christ and God's Word. Walk out your repentance with action. Ask the Holy Spirit to guide and empower you to do it!

Galatians 2:20 (NIV) I have been crucified with Christ and I no longer live, but Christ lives in me. The life I live in the body, I live by faith in the Son of God, who loved me and gave himself for me.

Ephesians 5:18 (NIV) "…be filled with the Spirit."

SPIRITUAL GIFTS LIST

Administration
The supernatural ability to organize tasks and people in a way that reflects the order and peace of heaven.
Scriptures: Acts 6:1—7; 1 Cor. 12:28

Apostle
The apostle is a person who carries a matured ministry of pioneering new ministries or churches and equips believers to do the same.
Scriptures: Rom. 1:5; 1 Cor. 12:28; 2 Cor. 12:12; Eph. 4:11—14

Craftsmanship
The supernatural ability to design, build and create through working with one's hands.
Scriptures: Exod. 30:22, 31:3—11: 2; Chr. 34:9—13; Acts 18:2—3

Discernment
The supernatural ability to spiritually identify the true nature of a matter, whether right or wrong, good or evil.
Scriptures: Matt. 16:21—23; Acts 5:1—11, 16:16—18; 1 Cor. 12:10

Evangelist
The evangelist is a person who carries a matured ministry of sharing the gospel of Christ with effect and equips believers to do the same.
Scriptures: Acts 8:5—6, 26—40, 14:21, 21:8; Eph. 4:11–14

Exhortation
The supernatural ability to motivate others to spiritual strength and action.
Scriptures: Acts 14:22; Rom. 12:8; 1 Tim. 4:13; Heb. 10:24—25

Faith
The supernatural ability to believe God for breakthrough results in a particular matter.
Scriptures: Acts 11:22—24; Rom. 4:18—21; 1 Cor. 12:9; Heb. 11

Giving
The supernatural ability to produce and generously share the wealth of one's time, money and reputation.
Scriptures: Rom. 12:8; 2 Cor. 8:1—7, 9:2—7

Healing
The supernatural ability to release God's power to heal, restore and deliver others from physical, emotional and spiritual bondage.
Scriptures: Acts 3:1—10, 9:32—35, 28:7—10; 1 Cor. 12:9, 28

Helps
The supernatural ability to come alongside individuals and teams in order to accomplish tasks and mission assignments.
Scriptures: Mark 15:40—41; Acts 9:36; Rom. 16:1—2; 1 Cor. 12:28

Hospitality
The supernatural ability to cultivate atmospheres that honor, welcome and communicate value to guests.
Scriptures: Acts 16:14—15; Rom. 12:13, 16:23; Heb. 13:1—2; 1 Pet. 4:9

Intercession
The supernatural ability to understand and pray for God's heart on a matter with effect.
Scriptures: Rom. 8:26—27

Interpretation
The supernatural ability to interpret a message in tongues so that others may understand and receive from God.
Scriptures: 1 Cor. 12:10, 14:1—14

Leadership
The supernatural ability to influence others through modeling the servant nature of Christ.
Scriptures: Rom. 12:8; 1 Tim. 3:1—13, 5:17; Heb. 13:17

Mercy
The supernatural ability to feel God's heart for the broken and to care for them.
Scriptures: Matt. 9:35—36; Mark 9:41; Rom. 12:8; 1 Thess. 5:14

Miracles
The supernatural ability to see alter natural outcomes by releasing God's kingdom into a matter.
Scriptures: Acts 9:36—42; 19:11—12, 20:7—12; Rom. 15:18—19; 1 Cor. 12:10, 28

Pastor/Shepherd
The pastor/shepherd is a person who carries a matured ministry of spiritually nurturing a group of people and equips others to do the same.
Scriptures: John 10:1—18; Eph. 4:1—14; 1 Tim. 3:1—7; 1 Pet. 5:1—3

Prophecy
The supernatural ability to hear God and share His word with others.
Scriptures: Acts 2:37—40, 7:51—53, 26:24—29; 1 Cor. 14:1—1; 1 Thess. 1:5

Prophet
The prophet is an individual who carries a matured revelatory ministry and equips other believers to hear God and share His word with others.
Scriptures: Acts 11:27—30, 15:32; Eph. 4:1—14

Teaching
The supernatural ability to communicate the truth of God's word with understanding and depth.
Scriptures: Acts 18:24—28, 20:20—21; 1 Cor. 12:28

Teacher
The teacher is an individual who carries a matured teaching ministry and equips others to communicate the truth of God's word with understanding and depth.
Scriptures: Acts 19:8—10; Eph. 4:11—14

Tongues
The supernatural ability to: 1) pray in a heavenly language to build oneself up in faith; 2) speak to others in their native tongue for the sake of the gospel. These are two different kinds of tongues from God.
Scriptures: Acts 2:1—13; 1 Cor. 12:10, 14:1—14; Jude 20

Word of Knowledge
The supernatural ability to receive information from God by spiritual means.
Scriptures: Acts 5:1—11; 1 Cor. 12:8; Col. 2:2—3

Word of Wisdom
The supernatural ability to receive insight from God to bring heavenly clarity, insight and direction to a matter.
Scriptures: Acts 6:3, 10; 1 Cor. 2:6—13, 12:8

#NewIdentity

For booking and more from
Adam Narciso, visit:

www.adamnarciso.com

To learn about Catalyst Ministries, visit:

www.catalystschool.com

CPSIA information can be obtained
at www.ICGtesting.com
Printed in the USA
LVHW08s2059191018
594174LV00005B/10/P